The Church Militant
and Iberian Expansion
1440-1770

THE JOHNS HOPKINS SYMPOSIA
IN COMPARATIVE HISTORY

The Johns Hopkins Symposia in Comparative History are occasional volumes sponsored by the Department of History at The Johns Hopkins University and The Johns Hopkins University Press, comprising original essays by leading scholars in the United States and other countries. Each volume considers, from a comparative perspective, an important topic of current historical interest. The present volume is the tenth. Its preparation has been assisted by the James S. Schouler Lecture Fund.

super iustos: & aures eius in preces eorum. Vultus autem domini super facientes mala: vt

perdat de terra memoriam eorum. Pſ. 33.

Oculi domini

From the Japanese translation of the Guia do Pecador (The Sinner's Guide) by Fr. Luís de Granado, O.P., published by the Jesuit Mission Press at Nagasaki in 1599. (From the collection of C. R. Boxer.)

The
Church Militant
and
Iberian Expansion
1440-1770

C. R. BOXER

THE JOHNS HOPKINS UNIVERSITY PRESS

Baltimore and London

The Johns Hopkins Symposia in Comparative History, no. 10

Copyright © 1978 by The Johns Hopkins University Press

Manufactured in the United States of America

The Johns Hopkins University Press, Baltimore, Maryland 21218
The Johns Hopkins Press Ltd., London

Library of Congress Catalog Number 77–18386
ISBN 0–8018–2042–1

Library of Congress Cataloging in Publication data will be found on the last printed page of this book.

Contents

Preface

When I was honored by the invitation to give these four Schouler Lectures in 1976, the chairman of the History Department wrote: ''I understand you have long been studying native clergies in the overseas empires of European powers. Thus I suggest the theme of 'Christianization of Non-European peoples in Africa, Asia, and the Americas; 1415–1825.' ''

In accepting this kind invitation, I made a shift of emphasis in the suggested theme. As can be seen from the book's title, the lectures focus on the aims and attitudes of the Portuguese and Spanish branches of the Roman Catholic church rather than on the views and actions of the papacy at Rome. Naturally, these two themes cannot be completely separated, and they were sometimes in harmony and sometimes in conflict. This constant tug and pull of opinions is, I trust, sufficiently documented in the text; but it could easily have been enlarged upon, had time and space permitted. Equally naturally, the format of a limited lecture series does not allow for a coverage which is all-embracing. I have therefore restricted myself to a consideration of four salient aspects of Portuguese and Spanish missionary enterprise.

The first chapter deals with the racial problems posed by the education and formation of an indigenous clergy among peoples of very different ethnic origins and cultural backgrounds from those of the Iberian peninsula. It shows how, after more than a century of almost complete indifference to this problem, the papacy began to press seriously for the ordination of suitable indigenous candidates for the priesthood, but commonly—though not invariably—met with obstruction from the representatives of the two Iberian crowns. It also touches on the controversial topic of black African slavery, contrasting the indifference of the papacy to the horrors of the West African slave trade with the outspoken protests of a few, if unrepresentative, individual Iberian clerics. The second chapter deals with the cultural problems involved in the presentation of Roman Catholic dogma to peoples who were totally ignorant of this religion. It also briefly discusses the missionaries' own varying reactions to the unknown and unfamiliar faiths which they encountered overseas. The third chapter is concerned with four key organizational problems: relations between the regular and the secular clergy; the mission as a frontier institution from Mexico to the Philippines; the two Iberian royal patronages (*padroado* and *patronato*) of the colonial church; the role of the Inquisition overseas. The fourth chapter discusses another three topics arising out of the first three chapters: the quality and quantity of the converts made by the missionaries of the Church Militant in Africa, America, and Asia; some specific instances of the persistance of idolatry and of synthetic Christianity; the flow and ebb of missionary élan, as reflected in the motives which inspired the spiritual *conquistadores* of the sixteenth century and those of their successors in the ensuing two hundred years.

The great majority of the Portuguese and Spanish missionaries were very conscious of being the vanguard of the Church Militant as well as loyal subjects of their respective crowns. Their convictions and their motives were not necessarily shared by their other European colleagues, although in many instances they were. But for better or for worse, the Iberian spiritual pioneers played a vital role in the overseas expansion of Europe which initiated the making of the modern world.

Acknowledgments

I am very grateful to the chairman and members of the Department of History at The Johns Hopkins University for inviting me to give the James S. Schouler Lectures in March 1976. I am equally grateful for the hospitality shown me on that occasion, and for the efficiency of the arrangements made by Professor John Russell-Wood. The lectures are published in the form in which they were delivered, but additional and illustrative documentation has been provided in the end notes.

CHAPTER ONE

Race Relations

Since the church's attitude to race relations is a vast, complex, and controversial topic, this chapter will focus on two principal aspects: (a) the indigenous clergy, and (b) Negro slavery.

The reasons for this choice are not far to seek. It was assumed by virtually all true believers during the period under consideration that the Holy Bible, on which the church's teaching was mainly based, was a divinely inspired work of universal validity for all times, for all places, and for all peoples. Consequently, if the church tolerated — or advocated — a color-bar, and if it made no objections to the "legitimate" enslavement of unbaptized Black Africans, there was no reason for laymen to have any qualms or doubts about such matters. Moreover, it is interesting to see how devout believers reacted on coming into close and continuous contact with races beyond the rim of Christendom, which were hitherto unknown (Amerindians on the other side of the Atlantic, Congolese in West Africa, Japanese in Asia) or which had been known only fleetingly and tenuously (Indian and Chinese) to medieval Europe. Attitudes and convictions formed as the Iberian mariners, missionaries, merchants, and men-at-arms spread around the globe lasted for centuries, and are still with us in varying degrees.

Race prejudice and black slavery were for centuries insepara-ble, in so far as the vast majority of western Europeans were concerned. The church might with one voice proclaim the brotherhood of all believers; but it might also implicitly or explicitly sanction a color-bar and slavery. When new or unfamiliar peoples were brought within the fold of Mother Church, why should many of them, even after the passage of several generations, find it difficult or impossible to become ordained priests? Why should others be "legitimately" enslaved for more than three centuries? This chapter does not provide all the answers, being concerned more with hard facts than with speculative theology. But it discusses some of the principal developments in this complex and controversial field, in which the pride and exclusiveness of the church were directly involved.

THE INDIGENOUS CLERGY

However desirable the development of an indigenous clergy may have been in theory, in practice such a clergy took a long time to develop in most countries outside Europe, and in some regions it never existed to any significant degree until very recent years. In many places and for long periods the formation of a responsible native clergy was opposed by those very missionaries who should have been in favor of it — an observation, incidentally, that applies to Protestants as well as to Roman Catholics. Whatever the theory may have been, in practice a colored indigenous clergy was apt to be kept in a strictly subordinate role to the white European priests, particularly where these latter were members of the religious orders — the regular clergy as opposed to the secular clergy. A rapid survey of developments in three continents during three centuries will show how this discrimination arose and the length of time for which it endured in the overseas regions controlled or claimed by the two Iberian crowns of Portugal and Castile, respectively.

West African Clergy

As a result of the Portuguese voyages of discovery and trade along the West African coast during the fifteenth century, many

West Africans were taken to Portugal, primarily as slaves, but some as freemen, or who were subsequently freed. A number of these latter received a religious training and education, the earliest recorded instance being that of a kidnapped black boy who was given to the Franciscan friars of São Vicente do Cabo in 1444, and who subsequently became a friar in that order— presumably a lay brother, although the chronicler who is our source remains vague on this point.[1] Zurara also tells us that next year another black youth was captured near the banks of the River Senegal, whom the Infante Dom Henrique educated in Portugal, apparently with the idea of sending him back to Africa as a missionary priest.[2] In the event, this Senegalese died before reaching manhood, but this precedent was followed up during the second half of the fifteenth century. We have no reliable figures showing how many actually returned to West Africa as catechists, priests, or interpreters; although the crown certainly envisaged that they should do so, particularly after cordial relations had been established with the Bantu kingdom of Congo during the reign of King John II of Portugal. The German physician, Jerome Münzer, who visited Portugal in 1494, where he was hospitably received by this monarch, states that he saw many black youths who had been, or who were being, educated in Latin and theology with the object of sending them back to the island of São Tomé, the kingdom of Congo and elsewhere as missionaries, as interpreters and as emissaries of King John II. Münzer adds: ''It seems likely that in the course of time, the greater part of Ethiopia [i.e., West Africa] will be converted to Christianity. Likewise two German printers went there [São Tomé], one of Nördlingen and the other of Strasbourg. Let us hope that they return safe and sound, since that region is not a healthy one for Germans.''[3]

The most famous of those Lisbon-educated African priests who did return to their homeland was Dom Henrique, a son of the great king Afonso I of Congo, who was consecrated as titular bishop of Utica by a rather reluctant Pope Leo X in 1518. He returned to the Congo capital, Mbanza Kongo—now called São

Salvador—in Northern Angola, in 1521, but he died there some ten years later after a long illness. It would seem that he had become too acclimatized during his long stay in Portugal, since he complained in 1526 that he had been unwell ever since his return to Africa and would like to return to Portugal. Even before his death, King Afonso had sent various young nephews and cousins to be educated as priests in Portugal, in the hope that two or three would likewise be consecrated bishops, as the Congo was too vast for one prelate to supervise adequately. It does not appear that any of them did attain the episcopal dignity, despite the statements of some Portuguese chroniclers implying that they did.[4] But it is certain that a steady trickle of noble Congolese youths continued to come to Lisbon for their education, which most of them received at the Lisbon monastery of Saint John the Evangelist, popularly known as Santo Eloi. The chronicler and humanist, João de Barros (c. 1496–1570), in his *Cartilha* of 1539, dedicated to the late Infante Dom Felipe, notes of the four Paravá headmen from Malabar who came to Lisbon then: "Your father [King John III] ordered them to be maintained in the monastery of Santo Eloi of this city, so that they can study there with the other Ethiopians from the Congo, from whom we have already formed bishops and theologians, certainly something very new in the Church of God, even though it is prophesied in Psalm 71."[5] A number of these Congolese youths died before they had completed their studies at Lisbon, and one of King Afonso's nephews chose to become a schoolmaster and a married man rather than return to Congo. But the way seemed open for the formation of a fully qualified indigenous clergy in two continents, with the promulgation of a papal Brief in June 1518, authorizing the royal chaplain at Lisbon to ordain "Ethiopians, Indians and Africans" who might reach the moral and educational standards required for the priesthood.[6]

It is obvious that at this period there was no color-bar involved in so far as the development of an indigenous clergy was concerned, whether African or Indian; but it was not long before racial prejudice made itself felt, although with varying intensity in time and place. The projected evangelization of the Bantu kingdom of Congo had foundered by the mid-sixteenth century, despite its promising start. This story is well known and I will not repeat it here.[7] Suffice it to remind you that this failure was largely due to the greater attractions of the West African slave trade, in which the missionaries (or some of them) became actively involved. Tropical diseases also decimated the European missionary personnel — never numerous in any event — thus militating against continuity of effort. Nevertheless, a small number of African and Asian students (*estudantes Indios e pretos*) continued to receive an education for the priesthood at Santo Eloi. Some of these evidently returned to their respective homelands, although references are very few and far between.[8]

The growth of race prejudice against persons of black African blood can mainly be accounted for by the development of the Negro slave trade, which received a great impetus during the sixteenth century with the demand for West African slaves in the Iberian colonies in the New World. The association of the Black African with chattel slavery goes back further than that, however, and we find and early instance in the *Travels* of the Bohemian knight, Leo of Rozmital, who visited Portugal in 1466. On taking leave of King Afonso V and his court, this monarch offered Rozmital anything that he would like as a present. The Bohemian asked for two Negro slaves, whereat the king's brother burst out laughing and said he should ask for something more valuable, as the Portuguese enslaved annually "a hundred thousand or more Ethiopians of both sexes, who are sold like cattle."[9] The number was a great exaggeration, as annual imports could hardly have amounted to a tenth of that figure; but the Duke of Viseu's remark indicates that the upper classes at any rate tended to regard Negro slaves in some respects as subhuman. Similarly, a strong racial prejudice against mulattos was not long in developing, even in the island of São Tomé, where they formed a high percentage of the population by the early sixteenth century. These critics took the common line, which has been reiterated so often since then, that persons of mixed blood inherited the vices rather than the virtues of their progenitors. Mulattos were repeatedly denounced as being "insolent, mischievous and difficult to manage." [10]

In the year 1571, a seminary for the training of local youths (*moços naturais da terra*) was opened at São Tomé by the Bishop (Fr. Gaspar Cão, 1554–74) of that island. Twenty-four years later it was reported that all the priests who were then active in the island had graduated from this seminary. Nevertheless, it had been closed in 1585 by Cão's successor (Dom Martinho de Ulhoa, 1578–91), on the grounds that the graduates were unsuitable and that it would be better to train them at Coimbra, for which purpose he purchased a house to serve as a seminary for them there. Ten years later, the next bishop (Dom Fr. Francisco de Vilanova, 1590–1602) reversed this policy, supporting the local citizens who petitioned the crown to reopen the seminary at São Tomé and close the one at Coimbra. They averred that this latter had never been used for the purpose for which it was intended, since it was very expensive for the islanders to send their sons to Portugal, and in any event the European climate did not agree with them. The crown, through its advisory board of Conscience and Orders, referred this petition to ex-Bishop Ulhoa for his opinion, and he urged that it should be rejected. He alleged that the pagan inhabitants of the West African mainland had no use nor respect for colored clergy and missionaries. They only wanted white evangelists, "whom they call the Sons of God." He added that the mulatto boys of São Tomé were by nature very viciously inclined and that they could only reach the required moral and intellectual standards if they were sent very young to Portugal and educated there until they were ordained. Rather than wasting time in trying to educate mulattos and Negroes for the priesthood, he affirmed, it would be better to send out to West Africa poor white clergy, who had no benefices or livings in Portugal, and to educate white orphan boys for the priesthood at the empty Coimbra seminary. The crown accepted Bishop Ulhoa's advice in the first place; but Bishop Vilanova seems to have gone ahead and reopened the São Tomé seminary in any event. He declared in 1597 that the graduates and ordinands formed a model clergy and that he had no trouble with them. His successors were mostly far less complimentary about the colored clergy of São Tomé; and in the early eighteenth century there was unedifying rivalry between the black and the mulatto canons of the cathedral chapter, in which both sides resorted to arms and appealed to Lisbon for support. [11]

The Cape Verde Islands, oldest of the European colonies in West Africa, were described by their disgruntled governor in 1627 as being "the dung-heap of the Portuguese empire." Such prosperity as they possessed was due to the inportance of the island of Santiago as an entrepôt for the West African slave trade. The Jesuits maintained a mission on that island and in Upper Guinea from 1604 to 1642, when they relinquished it, owing to the high death rate among their white personnel, and lack of an adequate financial base. The Cape Verde secular clergy, whom they trained during their stay there, was exclusively colored, winning a glowing eulogy from the celebrated Jesuit missionary Padre António Vieira, when the ship which was taking him to the Maranhão put into Santiago for a few days in December 1652. Vieira preached in the cathedral on Christmas Day, and wrote of the Dean and Chapter: "They are all black, but it is only in this respect that they differ from Europeans. There are here clergy and canons as black as jet, but so well bred, so authoritative, so learned, such great musicians, so discreet and so accomplished, that they may be envied by those in our own cathedrals at home." He urged his superiors in Portugal to re-establish the Jesuit mission, and he exhorted the local canons to volunteer for missionary work on the mainland. In neither respect was he successful; and although the Capuchins in 1656 took up the task abandoned by their Jesuit precursors, the seminary vegetated and standards declined disastrously in the second half of the eighteenth century. Of course, there were always honorable exceptions,

and at an earlier period a black priest named João Pinto won
high praise from many contemporaries for self-sacrificing
labors as a missionary in"the rivers of Guinea" during the late
sixteenth and early seventeenth centuries.[12]

The Portuguese conquest and occupation of coastal Angola
and their advance into the interior along some of the river
valleys, initiated in 1575, periodically brought the problem of
developing a native clergy to the attention of the authorities at
Lisbon. Apart from anything else, the mortality rates for
Europeans in the fever-stricken regions of West Africa were so
high that white Portuguese clergy were very reluctant to go
there. Accordingly, suggestions for establishing a seminary for
the training of black West African clergy, elsewhere than in São
Tomé and Santiago de Cabo Verde, were adumbrated from time
to time, though there were differences of opinion whether this
institution should be located in West Africa itself or in Europe.
In 1627–28, for example, the crown consulted the Jesuits at
Lisbon on the advisability of erecting one or more seminaries in
Portugal, specifically for the training and education of West
African youths, who would then be sent back to do missionary
and parish work in their own countries, as was still being done
on a small scale by the "Blue Canons" of Santo Eloi. The
Jesuits replied that such seminaries should be founded in
Angola rather than in Portugal itself, since this would be
cheaper for the crown and more convenient for the Africans.
They added that if the crown should decide to educate these
black students in Portugal, this should be done at Lisbon rather
than at either of the two university towns, Coimbra and Evora.
Black university students, they averred, would be unmercifully
teased and bullied by their white colleagues, and they would
also be tempted to lead unedifying lives. The Jesuits likewise
adduced the undesirable precedent of Irish boys educated in
Spain and Portugal, who were often reluctant to return to the
dangerous and uncomfortable Irish mission-field, but opted for
lucrative chaplaincies in noble Iberian households. The Jesuits
concluded that it would suffice to teach these African students

Latin and "cases of conscience," by means of what would nowadays be termed a "crash course" in basic theology. This would be sufficient for them to act effectively in the African mission-fields, and it would avoid the expense and delay of a lengthy and rigorous theological training. A few exceptionally gifted individuals might be admitted to Coimbra and Evora for higher education, and they might be given more responsible ecclesiastical positions after their return to West Africa, they conceded. But what the Jesuits suggested, in effect, was the formation of a second-rate African clergy. [13]

Proposals for the establishment of a seminary for training West African clergy on the African mainland, either at Luanda or at São Salvador do Congo, continued to be bandied back and forth between these two places and Lisbon throughout the seventeenth century. The crown, whether in the persons of the Spanish Habsburgs (1580–1640) or of the Portuguese Braganzas (after 1640), and the colonial bishops alike agreed in theory that an indigenous African clergy would be a good thing; but they argued interminably about whether it was best to educate students in Portugal or in Africa. In the upshot, the crown never came up with the money to endow a seminary on an adequate scale in either continent. The small Jesuit college at São Salvador, which functioned from 1625 to 1669, and their longer lived college at Luanda were both originally endowed by a wealthy ex-slave trader, Gaspar Alvares (*O menino diabo*, "the baby devil"), who became a lay brother in the Society after a shattering sexual experience. [14] While the Jesuits refused to admit either blacks or mulattos to their own ranks, they did train them at these colleges to enter the secular priesthood. A similar attitude was taken by the other religious orders which worked in the Congo and Angola, of whom the Italian Capuchins were the most effective from 1649 onward. A very few individual *mestiço* Jesuits and friars merely represented the proverbial swallows that do not make a summer. With the fragmentation of the Old Kindgom of Congo after the battle of Ambuila in 1665, missionary work became more difficult than ever. Christianity, though still widely professed, became increasingly Africanised. The black and mulatto clergy of São Salvador were the perennial targets of hostile criticism from the few white priests who ventured that far. [15]

Whatever criticisms were made of the colored clergy in West Africa, and the barrage of adverse criticism never ceased for over three centuries, the fact remained, as Bishop Oliveira of Angola pointed out in 1689, that such a clergy was indispensable, since the death rate among the whites was so high. West Africa's reputation as the "White Man's grave" was fully justified for many years, since the causes and cures of tropical diseases were not understood before the nineteenth and twentieth centuries. European-born clergy were singularly reluctant to go there, once the preliminary euphoria of converting the Congo kingdom had passed. Periodically, suggestions were made that they should be forced to go, like it or not. In 1644, for example, King John IV circulated the prelates in Portugal that they should dispatch thither their unwanted, unruly, or even convicted criminal clergy, who would then redeem their sins in the mission-field. Needless to say, nothing came of such desperate remedies; but they reflected a common conviction that it was better to have an immoral and inferior clergy, whether black or white, than none at all. [16]

East African Clergy

In striking contrast to the long-standing and persistent, if only partly successful, efforts to maintain an indigenous clergy in West Africa, we find nothing of the kind on the opposite coast. For over three centuries no Bantu clergyman was ever ordained in Mozambique, although it was suggested in 1694 and again in 1761 that efforts should be made to develop an indigenous clergy. But the Marquis of Pombal's dictatorial order that a seminary should be founded for this purpose on Mozambique island was quietly but effectively ignored by the authorities concerned. Not until 1875 was a seminary opened on that island, but it was closed two years later for lack of pupils. In

1954, Canon Alcantara Guerreiro, the ecclesiastical historian of Mozambique, sadly observed that not a single indigenous priest had yet been ordained in that province.

It is true that a very few blacks of East African origins were ordained at Goa or in Portugal in the sixteenth, seventeenth, or eighteenth centuries, but they worked in Portuguese India and did not return to the land of their birth. They included a Dominican friar, Fr. Miguel de Apresentação, the nephew and heir of the christianized "Emperor" of Monomotapa, who had been nominally converted to Christianity in 1629. Fr. Antonio Ardizone Spinola, an aristocratic Italian Theatine priest, who knew this black friar well at Goa in the 1640s, later reported: "Although he is a model priest, leading a very exemplary life, saying Mass daily, yet not even the habit which he wears secures him any consideration there, just because he has a black face. If I had not seen it, I would not have believed it." On the other hand, Fr. Miguel declined an invitation from his royal Bantu relatives to return to Monomotapa in 1650, preferring to remain at Goa, where he became Vicar of the Dominican priory of Santa Barbara in 1670, with a master's degree in theology, and where he died soon afterwards. [17] It was, perhaps, to Fr. Miguel, or else to one of his relatives, that the papal collector at Lisbon, Lorenzo Tramallo, was referring when he wrote to Cardinal Barberini at Rome in 1633, that a black African Dominican priest was leaving for Mozambique. He added: "I have always been strongly of the opinion that natives should be promoted to the priesthood, but nearly all our Europeans disapprove of this being done. However, I do not place so much reliance on them as on Saint Thomas [the Apostle], who placed his trust in Indian priests. These latter have kept the faith throughout the centuries, despite their distance from the Holy See." Whoever this black friar was, he did not get to Monomotapa. The colored clergy and friars of Mozambique, who were the target of so much hostile criticism by colonial governors and from officials for over two centuries, were either *mestiços*, or, more commonly, Goan secular clergy. [18]

Goan Clergy

In Portuguese India, a seminary for the education and training of an indigenous clergy was established at Goa in 1541. It was taken over by the Jesuits shortly afterward, and it remained under their control until the dissolution of the Portuguese branch of the Society of Jesus in 1759–61. This seminary of the Holy Faith, as it was originally called, was a multiracial institution in the fullest sense of the term. Boys of all races and classes were admitted, including a few Abyssinians and Bantu from East Africa, although Indians naturally predominated. The colored students who graduated from this seminary were ordained as secular priests, and only very rarely were they admitted to any of the religious orders before the second half of the eighteenth century. They were primarily used as catechists and auxiliaries to the European regulars, who likewise provided most of the parish priests during the same period. Moreover, these indigenous secular priests were deliberately recruited from the highest castes only; that is to say, from the more or less forcibly converted Brahmins (or *Brahmenes* as the Portuguese called them), and occasionally from the *Kshatriyas*, or warrior caste. The Indian Christians kept, and indeed still keep, their caste divisions and the ban on intermarriage between different castes, despite their conversion to Christianity. Yet most of the Portuguese ecclesiastical and secular authorities did not trust them; and some of the archbishops of Goa were singularly reluctant to ordain any Indians at all. One of these prelates, Dom Cristovão de Sá e Lisboa (1610–22), is said to have sworn on the Missal never to do so.[19]

The first breach in the theory and practice of white superiority in the ecclesiastical hierarchy of Portuguese India was effected when a Christian *Brahmene*, Mattheus de Castro, after being refused ordination by the archbishop of Goa, made his way overland to Rome in 1625. Here, he was not only ordained a priest, but, after completing his theological studies with great credit, he was consecrated bishop of Chrysopolis, *in partibus infidelium*, and later appointed vicar-apostolic of Bijapur. But although he was warmly supported by the cardinals of the Congregation of the Propaganda Fide at Rome, the Portuguese civil and ecclesiastical authorities at Goa refused to allow him to exercise his episcopal functions on their territory, claiming that the papal authorization which he carried had been obtained under false pretenses. His principal antagonist was the venerable Jesuit Patriarch of Ethiopia, Dom Affonso Mendes, who did not scruple to term his colleague of Chrysopolis "a bare-bottomed Nigger." The mutual denunciations of these two prelates remind one of Cunninghame Graham's jocose remark concerning the contemporary controversy between the Jesuits of Paraguay and their Franciscan Bishop Cardenas:"Hell has been said to have no fury equal to that of a woman scorned, but a bishop thwarted makes a very tolerable show."[20]

I may add that there were always a few Portuguese officials and clerics who spoke up in favor of the despised *Canarim* secular clergy, affirming that they were just as good, or even better, than the white Jesuits, Franciscans and other regulars who occupied most of the coveted ecclesiastical offices and benefices. These apologists included at least one Inquisitor, at Goa, the outspoken Pero Borges, who drew up a strongly worded memorial in their favor in 1650. Some of the archbishops also patronized and encouraged them, particularly those who were inclined to be hostile to the Jesuits, such as the haughty Dom Fr. António Brandão (1675–78). But the weight of Portuguese colonial official opinion was usually against them for the best part of three centuries. Both the secular and the ecclesiastical authorities were generally agreed that the *Brahmene* clergy should be kept in a subordinate position. Their opportunities and their status gradually improved during the first half of the eighteenth century, partly because of the remarkable achievements of the Goan priests of the Congregation of the Oratory of Santa Cruz (founded 1691), whose selfless devotion preserved the Roman Catholic community in Ceylon from collapsing under Dutch Calvinist persecution.[21] It is also significant that a

Brahmene priest, Lucas de Sa (1654–1717), was finally able to obtain several high ecclesiastical offices, including that of censor of the Inquisition at Goa, despite much opposition. [22] But generally speaking, the Goan or *Canarim* clergy continued to be relegated to a strictly subordinate role, mainly because of racial prejudice against them, until the closing years of the dictatorship of the Marquis of Pombal, 1761–77. This quirky Jekyll-and-Hyde character, who combined many of the sentiments of the Enlightenment with the most ferocious forms of despotism, made energetic and largely successful efforts to ensure that the indigenous clergy of Portuguese Asia should achieve full equality with those of European origin, both in theory and in practice. [23]

If the Goan secular clergy in Portuguese India was for long kept in a strictly subordinate position and in an inferior status by the European-born ecclesiastical hierarchy, at least this indigenous clergy was both numerous and firmly established by the mid-seventeenth century. The same applies, to a lesser extent, to the black West African clergy. This was more than could be said of the regions under the sway of the Castilian crown's royal patronage (*patronato*), where an indigenous clergy was either nonexistent, or else had only achieved a much more limited development.

Colored Clergy in Spanish America

As had happened with the Portuguese on the other side of the world, the religious orders working in Spanish America from 1523 onward, originally had no racial discrimination against the admission of Amerindians and Africans in their respective constitutions, but by the end of the sixteenth century they had very rigid ones. Recalling early Portuguese efforts to educate Congolese and other West Africans for the priesthood, a senior colonial official, Rodrigo de Albornoz, advised the crown of Castile from Mexico City in 1525: "In order that the sons of *Caciques* [chiefs] and native lords may be instructed in the Faith, Your Majesty must needs command that a College be founded wherein there may be taught reading, grammar, philosophy, and other Arts, to the end that they may be ordained priests. For he who shall become such among them, will be of greater profit in attracting others to the Faith than will fifty [European] Christians.'' [24]

This and similar suggestions led to the founding of the College of Santiago de Tlateloco by Viceroy Mendoza and Bishop Zumarraga in 1536, which was entrusted to the management of the Franciscans. The pupils were limited to the sons of the indigenous Mexican aristocracy and a few mestizos. The college was primarily expected to serve the dual purpose of forming a cultural élite who would act as interpreters and a bond between conquerors and conquered, with the possibility of eventually admitting some of the best graduates to minor orders or even, perhaps, to the priesthood. This institution very soon aroused hostile criticism. The Dominican Provincial of Mexico trenchantly denounced the idea of forming a native clergy in 1544. He argued that Amerindians were mentally and racially inferior to Europeans, besides being potentially unreliable and too young in the Faith. His attitude rapidly obtained widespread support; and in 1555, the first Mexican Ecclesiastical Provincial Council declared that holy orders were not to be conferred on Amerindians, mestizos, and mulattos, who were classed with the descendants of ''Moors'' [i.e., Muslims], Jews, and persons who had been sentenced by the Inquisition, as being inherently unworthy of the sacerdotal office. The Second Provincial Council reinforced this wholly negative attitude. The Third Provincial Council (1585) relaxed this rigid prohibition slightly by forbidding that ''Mexicans who are descended in the first degree from Amerindians, or from Moors, or from parents of whom one is a Negro, be admitted to holy orders without great care being exercised in their selection.'' This left the door ajar for the admission of certain categories of people with mixed blood, as we shall see below, but implied the maintenance of the ban on full-blooded Amerindians and blacks. [25]

As regards the Viceroyalty of Peru, which covered the whole of the South American continent, save for Brazil and Guianas, the Second Ecclesiastical Provincial Council of Lima (1567–68) categorically forbade the ordination of Amerindians, but the Third Council (1582–83), implicitly relaxed this prohibition by stating that the rules laid down by the Council of Trent for the ordination of candidates for the priesthood must be strictly observed.[26] In effect, however, the original bans on the ordinations of full-blooded Amerindians remained in force for most of the colonial period, since they were legally classified as being *gente miserable* ("wretched people"). Originally, mulattos, blacks, and Afro-Amerindian racial groups were also included in this last category; but by the eighteenth century it became the practice, if not the theory, to include these mixed bloods as *gente de razón* ("sensible people"), leaving the Amerindians alone with the invidious distinction of being *gente apartada de razón*. The position regarding mestizos was more complicated. In the early years of the colonization of Hispaniola the Castilian crown had actively encouraged intermarriage between Spaniards and Amerindians, and there were no legal bars of any kind against mestizos. But the steady growth of mestizo communities was soon accompanied by a growth in racial prejudice against them, particularly after the 1540s, when the first generation of mainland mestizos was reaching adulthood in the vast viceroyalties of Mexico and Peru. Most of them were illegitimate, and this presumed defect rubbed off on the others, to the extent that in 1568 a royal decree prohibited mestizos from being ordained "for many reasons."

Protests by well-born mestizos and their influential Spanish fathers, particularly in Peru, led to some modification of this ruling, first at Rome and then at Madrid. After much backing, filling and contradictory legislation, the Castilian crown declared in 1588 that mestizos could be ordained, provided that they were of legitimate birth and that a most searching examination revealed that they possessed all the qualifications laid down by the Council of Trent for the conferment of holy orders.[27] Mulattos, due to the association of one or more of their forebears with Negro chattel slavery, were more sharply discriminated against, both socially and legally.

The thinking which lay behind these attitudes is best exemplified by the *De Procuranda Indorum salute* ('On the Preaching of
the Gospel in the Indies') by the influential Jesuit, José de
Acosta (1540–1600), who had worked for fourteen years in Peru
and for a year in Mexico. In this work (written 1577, published
1588), Acosta explains that it would be dangerous to confer holy
orders on the Amerindians, who were members of a race which
was so young in the Faith, quoting biblical and classical
precedents by way of justification (bk. 6, chap. 19). He admits
that he had been originally in favor of ordaining mestizos in
considerable numbers, since they were bilingual and could
explain the mysteries of faith to the Amerindians without
needing interpreters. But experience had shown that the great
majority of mestizos were individuals of ill repute and bad
character, as a result of being suckled at the breasts of
Amerindian mothers and brought up in close contact with that
inferior race. Here again, Acosta invoked biblical precedents in
justification of race prejudice, adducing Abraham's refusal to
let his son Isaac marry a Cananite woman, and Rebecca's mortal
disgust at the prospect of her son Jacob's marriage with a
daughter of Heth. He added, for good measure, St. Paul's
denunciation of the Cretans as "always liars, evil beasts, slow
bellies." Acosta ended by taking the same line as the crown's
decree of 1588 (which he had, perhaps, helped to inspire), by
stressing that although mestizos could be ordained, they should
only be so in very limited numbers and after rigorous selection,
screening and training.[28]

The advocates of the formation of an indigenous clergy
likewise quoted biblical precedents to bolster their case. They
argued that since Jews and Gentiles who were newly converted
to the Faith in the primitive church had been ordained as
priests, and even consecrated as bishops, the same privileges
should be extended to the sons of Asians, Africans, and
Amerindians, who had been baptized as infants and who were
of legitimate birth and otherwise well qualified. They could and
did instance the papal Brief of 1518 (p. 4 above) which

authorized the ordination of qualified Africans and Indians. For these men knew the native languages better and could preach more acceptably in them. Moreover, the people would then receive the Gospel at the lips of their own brothers more freely than from foreigners.

In so far as these and similar arguments were advanced for ordaining Amerindians, they were most emphatically repudiated by the great majority of missionary-friars and diocesan prelates. As Fr. Geronimo de Mendieta, O.F.M., explained in his *Historia Ecclesiastica Indiana* of 1599: "The majority of them are not fitted to command or to rule, but to be commanded or ruled. I mean to say that they are not fitted for masters but for pupils, not for prelates but for subjects, and as such they are the best in the world."[29] This attitude reflects the Aristotelian theory of the natural inferiority of some races to others—a theory which was very popular with the great majority of Iberian missionaries and *conquistadores*, or, for that matter, with their Dutch, French, and Anglo-Saxon successors as empire builders with "dominion over palm and pine" and over "lesser breeds without the law."

By the end of the sixteenth century, the position was, in effect, that Amerindians were not being ordained at all, and mestizos only very sparingly. Canonically the crown had no right to legislate in such a matter; but the papacy for a long time had neither the will nor the power to challenge what was done in the sphere of the Castilian crown's ecclesiastical patronage (*patronato, patronazgo*). However, by virtue of their episcopal office, the colonial bishops had wide powers to grant dispensations from all canonical irregularities, save only those of willful murder and simony. It is clear from the correspondence between the crown, the viceroys and the colonial prelates during the seventeenth century, that some bishops used their dispensing powers rather freely, whereas others were far more rigid.[30] In 1657, for example, the crown severely reprimanded the bishop of Tucumán for ordaining practically anybody who presented himself, irrespective of the candidate's color, birth, and educational qualifications. On the other hand, the bishop of Gua-manga, wrote on the 1 February 1626: "Ever since I officiated in this bishopric, I have not ordained any mestizos nor appointed them as parish priests of Indians, nor will I do so in the future." Don Juan Palafox y Mendoza, the celebrated archbishop of Puebla de Los Angeles and *interim* viceroy of Mexico in 1642, tells us in his privately printed *Virtudes del Indio* of 1650 that he personally knew in Mexico City a full-blooded Amerindian, Don Fernando, son and grandson of *caciques*, "who had been ordained and who made a very satisfactory priest." Unfortu-nately, he does not tell us his surname; but this individual was certainly very much of a *rara avis*.

In 1668, the archbishop of Quito, Fr. Alonso de la Peña Montenegro (1596–1687), published at Madrid a guide for parish priests in Spanish America *Itinerario para parochos de Indios*, which at once became and remained a standard *vade-mecum* on the subject, with several later editions during the next 150 years. He argued forcefully that Amerindians "are not deprived by birth or by blood of the right to receive holy orders." Ignoring or contradicting much crown and colonial legislation against their being allowed to do so, he urged that: "on the contrary, they should be encouraged and invited to do so, always provided that they are individuals who are also endowed with the aptitude and qualities necessary for an office so sublime," as enacted by the Council of Trent. He emphasized that mestizos could also be ordained without a dispensation being required, provided they were of legitimate birth and otherwise fully qualified. As regards ordaining blacks, he was positively revolutionary. He admitted that some canonists were against their ordination, "because for a Negro to go up to the altar to celebrate Mass would cause considerable consternation among white people whose contact with Negroes is limited to those who perform the meanest offices and who are for the most part slaves. But many other authorities, and weighty ones, are of the opinion that this does not in any way constitute an impediment to their being ordained; for in this part of the world where they are so numerous, and where some of them command troops and hold other military commissions, their becoming priests will be in no way disturbing: on the contrary, it has been our experience with the few who have actually received orders that the people have been much edified by them.'' Unfortunately, he does not identify the ''weighty authorities'' who advocated the ordination of Negroes, nor where the few Negro priests whom he met had been ordained. Probably they hailed from the Caribbean region, where blacks in the militia were by this time fairly numerous. In any event, despite the popularity of his book, his pleas for forming an indigenous clergy, whether Amerindian or black, were not followed up. Moreover, it is evident that he did not contemplate the ordination of Amerindian priests on anything but a very modest scale. In the same chapter in which he recommended that some should be ordained (bk. 2, treat. 1, sec. 1), he sweepingly condemned the vast majority of Amerindians for their inherent and ineradicable coarse barbarity (*bronca barbaridad*). They were temperamentally incapable of grasping the higher Christian truths; and they were congenitally cowardly, idle, drunken, and lazy. ''In short, they are a wretched race'' (*finalmente son gente miserable*).[31]

A great contrast to Montenegro de la Peña's attitude was that of his Creole colleague, the Lima-born archbishop of Caracas, Don Fray Antonio González de Acuña. This prelate, when officiating at an ordination ceremony in his cathedral in 1681, publicly declared: ''that it was not his intention to ordain any of those present who might be of Amerindian or Mulatto descent to the fourth generation; and in the very act of laying his hands on each candidate, he repeated his declaration that he would not and was not ordaining any *Mestizo*, Mulatto, or one of the Castes [mixed bloods].'' This declaration aroused great consternation among some of the faithful as to the validity of the sacraments they had previously received, ''suspecting that several of the priests who had ministered to them were not of the white race.'' The problem was referred to Madrid and to Rome, where it was examined by the Sacred College of the

Council in the Eternal City. Here it was decided that although the orders conferred by the archbishop on any colored man on that particular occasion were invalid, since he had expressly declared his intention of only ordaining whites, yet all prelates in the Indies should be told that henceforth they must not ordain anybody conditionally (*sub conditione*). Those ecclesiastics concerned must be reminded that there was, canonically, nothing to prevent Negroes and Amerindians, or their descendants from being ordained in holy orders, always provided that the candidates possessed in all other respects the qualifications laid down by canon law and the Council of Trent. [32]

After some hesitation, this papal ruling was accepted by the government at Madrid, but it was certainly not widely promulgated in the Indies. It is true that the crown by a royal decree of 12 July 1691 envisaged the foundation of College-seminaries in Mexico City and elsewhere, which would reserve a quarter of the places in each of them for the sons of Amerindian chiefs; an injunction repeated in another *cédula real* nearly six years later (22 March 1697). Nothing much seems to have come of these rulings nor of the crown's approval in 1685 of the bishop of Chiapas' project for founding a small *Colegio Seminario* at Guatemala, which would admit eight Amerindian students, sons of caciques. Typically, the crown at the same time renewed its ban on the ordination of mestizos and mulattos, despite the recent papal ruling in their favor. In 1706, the Archbishop of Santo Domingo, where the bulk of the population was by now of colored blood, asked the crown for permission to ordain a few mulattos, while restricting their possibilities of promotion. The royal sanction was given on this condition. [33]

The piecemeal, confusing, and contradictory nature of much crown and ecclesiastical legislation; the indifference often displayed by Rome to the color problems of the colonial clergy; the difficulty of implementing papal briefs, constitutions and decrees in the Indies; the race prejudices of the *Peninsulares* and the Creoles against the colored: all these factors combined to prevent the development of a broad-based indigenous clergy in

Spanish America until it was too late. In 1769, finally and firmly reversing its hesitant and uncertain stand of centuries, the Castilian crown sent categorical orders to all prelates in Spanish America and the Philippines that they must admit up to one-third or one-quarter of Amerindians, mestizo, or Filipino candidates for the priesthood in all the existing seminaries, and in those which might be established in the future. This requirement was formally embodied in the decisions of the Sixth Ecclesiastical Provincial Council held at Lima in 1772. But the decisions of this Council never received formal approval from either the king or the pope, so they never acquired the force of law. They did reflect the changing climate of opinion fostered largely by the Enlightenment; but no widespread attempt was made to enforce them before the whole situation was compromised by the outbreak of the Wars of Independence.[34] Indeed, the governor-general of the Philippines, writing to the crown in 1787, stated flatly that he had no intention of removing some Peninsular and Creole religious from their parishes (*doctrinas*) to make way for Filipino or Chinese-mestizo priests, even if the latter possessed the necessary canonical qualifications, as he had been ordered to do. The loyalty of the colored clergy could not be relied upon, he averred, and the experience of over two centuries had shown that Spanish domination in the Philippines directly depended on the Peninsular and Creole missionary-friars who administered the *doctrinas*.[35] This was the nub of the matter in the frontier regions of Spanish America as well. The colonial clergy in Spanish America and the Philippines therefore remained overwhelmingly Peninsular and Creole in composition, though more so in some regions than in others where a few Amerindians, Filipinos, or mestizos were admitted to subordinate roles.

Turning now to regions where the European intruders had to obey the existing laws and could not impose their own, as they could in the colonial world, we may glance very briefly at developments in mission-fields of Japan, China, and Vietnam, to take them in the chronological order in which they were opened.

Japanese Clergy

The Jesuit Japan Mission was founded by St. Francis Xavier in 1549. Progress at first was unavoidably slow, but thirty years later there may have been as many as 100,000 converts. There was no native clergy; and those Japanese who were admitted to the Society of Jesus could not aspire to become more than catechists and humble lay brothers. Francisco Cabral, the Portuguese Superior of the mission for over a decade (1570–81) had at one time envisaged the formation of an indigenous clergy, but he later reversed this attitude, making pejorative observations about the Japanese national character like: "But of course, that's a Japanese for you!", or "After all, they are Niggers, and their customs are barbarous." Like many Europeans before and since, Cabral stigmatised the Japanese as being an inconstant and unreliable race: "Believe me, Your Reverence, everything is quite different here. First of all, they do not have the natural disposition necessary [for vocations for the priesthood]. Then, too, it is on account of the climate of the country and the influence of the stars, since it seems as if an incessant restlessness and a constant desire for change holds the heart of these people." [36]

Cabral was relieved of his post by the celebrated Italian Jesuit Visitor, Alexandro Valignano, who speedily perceived the need for forming an indigenous clergy and admitting Japanese to the priesthood in the Society of Jesus. [37] His efforts were ably seconded and continued by the first resident Jesuit Bishop of Japan, Luís de Cerqueira, who administered his diocese from Nagasaki during sixteen troubled years, 1598–1614. But partly owing to causes beyond the Jesuits' control, and partly on account of hesitation, opposition, and misgiving within the Society itself, the seminary for training indigenous clergy only opened its doors in 1601 with an enrolment of eight students (two Portuguese mestizos and six Japanese). Only seven Japanese graduates had been ordained as secular (diocesan) priests when the prohibition of Christianity and the start of the Tokugawa government's persecution forced the seminary to

close thirteen years later, by which time there were also seven
Japanese Jesuit priests.[38] Considering the obstacles encountered by the founders and supporters of the seminary, this was a
far from negligible result; but as the history of the church in the
ensuing period of persecution showed, it was in the upshot a
classic instance of too little and too late.

Chinese Clergy

In China, after an even slower and a still more hesitant start,
the indigenous clergy in the long run fared rather better. St.
Francis Xavier had died on the island of Sanchian in the South
China Sea in December 1552, and Matteo Ricci had founded the
Jesuit Mission at Peking in 1601; but the first Chinese priest, Lo
Wen-tsao (*alias* Gregorio Lopez), was not ordained until 1654.
This was done by the Dominicans at Manila, and the first Jesuit
Chinese priest, the Macao-born Manuel de Siqueira (Cheng Ma-
no Wei-hsin), was not ordained until ten years later at Coimbra.
Despite the good work done by both these indigenous priests in
mainland China during the closing stages of a persecution
which had begun in 1664 when they were the only missionaries
who could — and did — circulate freely, many of their European
colleagues remained very hesitant about the advisability of
forming an indigenous Chinese clergy. Some Europeans were in
favor of ordaining Chinese who had a really good knowledge of
Latin (Sequeira was the sole individual with this qualification in
1668). Others were in favor of ordaining elderly Chinese catechists of proved virtue, even if they had little or no knowledge of
Latin, provided that Rome allowed the use of the liturgy in
Chinese. Yet others, including the majority of the Portuguese
Jesuits, were against ordaining any Chinese for the foreseeable
future. This third group considered the Chinese to be inherently
"full of vices, irresolute, and inconstant," just as Francisco
Cabral had said of the Japanese nearly a century earlier. These
critics argued that indigenous Chinese priests, through their
(alleged) immorality and greed of gain would ruin themselves
and the European missionaries as well.[39]

Those Europeans who were in favor of admitting Chinese to the priesthood, used much the same arguments as had the pioneer sixteenth-century Franciscan friars in Mexico who advocated, if only briefly, the same privilege for Amerindians. We may take as the Jesuit spokesman, the Belgian François de Rougemont (1601–76). To those of his colleagues who claimed that the Chinese were inherently unfit for the sublime sacerdotal office, he retorted that maybe some individuals were, but were the Cretans ''little saints?''—an echo of St. Paul's denunciation of those islanders as 'liars and slow bellies.'' Were the Ethiopians and the Indians invariably so firm? Were there not proud and corrupt people in Europe? The Anglians were regarded as barbarians by the Romans, but exemplary priests and bishops were recruited from them—an echo of Pope Gregory the Great's *non Angli sed Angeli*. Nor was it an adequate excuse to say that the work of conversion could not succeed until the emperor of China became a Christian, and the secular arm could be employed to support the ecclesiastical. For three centuries the early church could not rely on the secular arm, but she ordained indigenous priests in Europe none the less. The church should now do the same in China, while awaiting the appearance of a Chinese Constantine.

Rougemont further observed, truly enough, that the experience of eighty years had shown that many catechists and converts remained steadfast under torture and persecution. If there had been some apostates, there was also a Judas among the apostles. Touching on a more tender point, he observed that one objection to the formation of an indigenous clergy was that the European missionaries would eventually lose the controlling authority which they now held. Though he did not say so, a similar objection had been made to the formation of a native clergy in Japan, but had been overruled by the Visitor Alexandro Valignano. ''Are we, then,'' Rougemont asked rhetorically and reproachfully, ''more concerned with maintaining our authority than with maintaining and spreading the Faith?''[40]

The differences of opinion among the European missionaries in China, whether Jesuits, Franciscans, Dominicans, or the

later arrivals from the Propaganda Fide at Rome and the
Missions Étrangères of Paris, as to whether Chinese should be
ordained, and, if so, from what social background and in what
numbers, continued for another two centuries. This problem
was complicated by the related question of whether a Chinese
liturgy should be allowed, and , if so, to what scope and extent.
There were also deep cleavages of opinion over the toleration or
otherwise of the Chinese rites—forms of ancestor-worship and
of respect paid to Confucius. These divisions of opinion among
the missionaries in the field were reflected in the shifts and
hesitations of the policy makers at Rome and of successive popes
themselves. As an inevitable result, progress in forming an
indigenous Chinese clergy continued to be fitful and slow.
There may have been something between 200,000 and 300,000
Christians in China at the beginning of the eighteenth century,
although the lower figure is probably nearer the mark. These
were served by just over a hundred priests belonging to various
orders and institutions; but only four or five of these men were
Chinese, the remainder being Europeans. [41]

In 1739, there were still only eighteen Chinese priests working
in mainland China, as compared to a total of seventy-six
European missionaries. Subsequently, periodic persecutions
involving the arrest and deportation—but seldom the execution
—of European missionaries, gradually altered the balance in
favor of the indigenous clergy, by making the need for them
more obvious. In 1810, the Roman Catholic mission in China
counted 113 priests, of whom thirty-five were Westerners. This
left the native clergy at long last with a substantial majority; but
no Chinese had been consecrated a bishop since Gregory Lo
(also Lopez; Lo Wen-tsao) had been raised to that dignity in
1685.

Nor did many of the European missionaries lose their conviction of cultural and racial superiority over their Chinese colleagues during the eighteenth century. They preserved this
superiority complex even though they depended to an increasing degree on the support of their Chinese catechists and

coworkers. Unsurprisingly, the latter sometimes resented this, although we have very little information about the Chinese clergy from their own pens, as contrasted with the voluminous correspondence, published and unpublished, of the European missionaries. One of the few exceptions is afforded by the journal of André Ly.[42] Educated for fifteen years at the General College of Siam, maintained by the Société des Missions Étrangères as a seminary for educating Asian clergy, principally Chinese and Indochinese, he was ordained in 1725. Returning to China, he worked there for over fifty years, mostly in Fukien and Szechwan, until his death in 1774. During this time, he kept a journal in Latin, covering the years 1747–63. He confided to his journal that on one occasion in the presence of the papal legate, Cardinal de Tournon, all the European missionaries had complained of the pride, inconstancy and ingratitude of the Chinese, stigmatizing them as inherently unfit for the sacerdotal vocation. He added that thirty years later, the procurator of the Missions Étrangères at Canton, Antoine Conain, said much the same thing. During the periodic persecutions of the eighteenth century, the desirability of consecrating Chinese bishops was regularly discussed at Rome. These discussions were as regularly dropped when the persecutions in due course subsided, and the European priests and vicars-apostolic were once again in a better position to exercise and to retain their authority.

Vietnamese Clergy

There were no native bishops in Indochina during the period with which we are concerned; but the indigenous Vietnamese clergy in course of of time attained a relatively better position vis-à-vis their European colleagues than was the case in Japan, China, and the Philippines. This was especially true of Tongking, or North Vietnam — for that country then and for long after was divided between North and South prior to its unificaion by the Emperor Gia-long in July 1802. The southern half was usually styled Cochin-China by Europeans, although this term had originally been applied to the North.

The success of the Roman Catholic missions in the two
Vietnams, despite the fact that there never was in either
kingdom a monarch who patronised the European missionaries
to the extent that the K'ang-hsi Emperor did in China, may be
ascribed to several causes. Two remarkable French missionaries, the Jesuit Alexandre de Rhodes (1591–1660), and François
Pallu, titular bishop of Heliopolis and vicar-apostolic of Tongking
(1626–84) were mainly responsible for establishing the Vietnamese mission on firm foundation in the seventeenth century.
They both shared a deep conviction that it was essential to
establish, foster, and encourage a strongly rooted indigenous
clergy. They organized the Vietnamese male catechists, and
their female counterparts termed the *Amantes de la Croix*
("Lovers of the Cross"), in very tightly organized and rigor-
ously disciplined communal groups, solemnly vowed to poverty,
chastity, and obedience. The exceptionally high standards de-
manded from these catechists clearly attracted converts of
exceptional fervor. The result was that the Vietnamese catchists
became the backbone of the mission to an even greater extent
than their Chinese and Japanese colleagues did in their respective countries—which is saying a great deal. They were also
given some elementary medical training, enabling them to
function as "barefoot doctors" and to gain ready access to all
towns and villages. The success of these catechists can be
gauged from the fact that they kept the Vietnamese Christian
communities of some 300,000 converts in being at a time (July
1658) when only two European priests were allowed in Tongking.[43]

Although Europeans and Vietnamese got off to a good start in
close and cordial cooperation under the guidance of the dynamic
Alexandre de Rhodes, some European missionaries for long
remained hesitant about ordaining indigenous clergy in any
considerable numbers. Their doubts were not shared by François
Pallu, who vainly urged Rome to allow the consecration of
several Vietnamese bishops. Nine Tongkingese priests were

ordained in 1659–69, and thereafter progress was more rapid in both North and South Vietnam. Rivalry between the Portuguese Jesuit missionaries of the *Padroado* and the French missionaries of the M.E.P. and the vicars-apostolic also complicated things. But in 1689 the Jesuits formally agreed ''strongly to urge all the Christians to pay the proper respect due to the priests of their own race, . . . and they must be forbidden to speak contemptuously of them, for fear lest such contempt will rebound on the Vicars-Apostolic, who have ordained them after having examined them and tested their virtues for some years.''

Despite intermittent bouts of persecution, some of them severe, the North Vietnam mission in 1737 contained some 250,000 Christians in a country which was about half the size of France. Of these converts, some 120,000 belonged to the Portuguese Jesuits of the Province of Japan, who comprised four European Jesuits, three Vietnamese Jesuits, and three Vietnamese secular priests. The M.E.P. ministered to some 80,000 Christians with four European priests and sixteen Vietnamese. The Five Italian barefeet Augustinians of the Propaganda Fide had about 30,000 converts, and the four Spanish Dominicans from Manila about 20,000; both of these orders having more Vietnamese priests than European. These statistics make an interesting comparison with those for China in 1739, when there were about 120.000 Chinese converts and seventy-six European missionaries but only eighteen Chinese priests.

Siam and Cambodia

In the neighboring kingdoms of Cambodia and Siam, Hinayana Buddhism (with a strong tincture of Hinduism in the case of Cambodia) proved much more resistant to Christian missions than did the Mahayana Buddhism of the more sinified Vietnam. Thanks largely to the efforts of François Pallu, the M.E.P. maintained a flourishing seminary in Siam for educating indigenous priests from China and Southeast Asia. This institution survived the extinction of French political influence at Bangkok

and Ayuthia in the bloody aftermath of the Constantine Phaul-
khon episode in 1688; but Siamese, and for that matter Burmese,
converts were always very few and far between.

Cambodia, although regarded as a very peripheral and unim-
portant mission-field in comparison with China and the two
Vietnams, where the main missionary efforts were concentrated,
does, however, provide a curious instance of European racial
arrogance and cultural cocksureness. Two Franciscan missionaries, Bishop Valerius Rist and Fr. Serafino Maria de Borgia,
founded a modest mission in Cambodia in 1724. They obtained a
highly favorable *chapa* or authorization from the king, the terms
of which were dictated by themselves. They included the
stipulations that not only could they make converts freely
among all classes and build churches wherever they chose, but
that they would have complete and exclusive jurisdiction over
all their converts, including the right to ''compel them to keep
their religion by inflicting punishments and penalties.'' Probably
the Khemer king never intended to implement this concession
wholeheartedly, and the two Franciscans were sternly rebuked
by the Archbishop of Goa for their intrusion into a mission-field
claimed by the Portuguese *Padroado*. But the incident shows
the lengths to which some representatives of the Church
Militant would go when they thought that they could get away
with it. [44]

THE CHURCH AND NEGRO SLAVERY

The church's attitude to Negro slavery was, to put it politely,
a highly permissive one for nearly four centuries. The series of
papal Bulls authorizing and encouraging Portuguese expansion,
which were promulgated at the request of that crown between
1452 and 1456, gave the Portuguese a wide latitude in subduing
and enslaving any pagan peoples they might encounter if these
were ''inimical to the name of Christ.'' The Portuguese took full
advantage of these Bulls and they had developed a flourishing

West African slave trade by 1460. We have seen that the Duke of Viseu boasted in 1466 that West Africans of both sexes and all ages were bought and sold "like cattle" in the slave markets at Lisbon and Oporto. A papal Brief of 7 October 1462 is sometimes cited as evidence that the papacy condemned the African slave trade; but this document merely threatens with censures those who kidnapped, bought or sold *Christian* converts in the Canary Islands and in Guinea. It neither states nor implies any condemnation of enslaving pagans. Similarly, various Briefs and Bulls cited by clerical (and other) apologists as denouncing the Negro slave trade, turn out, on examination, to do nothing of the sort. They relate to the Luso-Brazilian *Paulistas*, who raided the Jesuit Reductions of Paraguay in the seventeenth and eighteenth centuries; and whose slaving activities, exclusively directed against Amerindians, aroused papal condemnation at the prompting of the Spanish Jesuits.[45]

It might be thought that the wording of the Bull *Sublimis Deus* promulgated by Pope Paul III in June 1537, though primarily directed against the enslavement of Amerindians, could be taken to include Africans and Asians as well, since one passage reads: "The said Indians and all other people who may later be discovered by Christians, are by no means to be deprived of their liberty or the possession of their property, even though they be outside the faith of Jesus Christ."[46] But neither the papacy itself nor the crowns of Castile and Portugal drew any such inference from it, nor was the validity of the earlier pro-Portuguese Bulls of 1452–56 in any way impugned thereby. The church itself was, and continued to be, a slave-holding institution on a massive scale in the Iberian colonial empires. Not only so, but for centuries the stipends of the bishop and the ecclesiastical establishment of Angola were financed from the proceeds of the slave trade.[47] Negro slaves were employed on Jesuit (and other) sugar plantations in Spanish and Portuguese America, as well as in domestic servitude there and in the Philippines, and in Portuguese Asia and Africa. Moreover, when the church did bring itself belatedly to denounce the enslavement of "civilized" races such as the Japanese and Chinese, it never explicitly nor implicitly extended such condemnation to the blacks of Africa. The papal Bulls of 1452-56, which explicitly authorized the enslavement of West African Negroes, were still being quoted in print as canonically valid by the "enlightened" bishop of Pernambuco, José Joaquim da Cunha de Azeredo Coutinho, in his defense of the Portuguese African slave trade in 1798–1806.[48]

Admittedly, there were always a very few maverick individuals who *did* condemn the African slave trade as being inherently unjustifiable, unchristian, and immoral. They included Bartolomé de Las Casas himself; but he only did so late in his life and without publicizing this retraction of his original advocacy of Negro slavery. His belated change of viewpoint therefore exerted no influence whatsoever, since it was not discovered, or at any rate not publicized, until the nineteenth century. The only prominent prelate who condemned the African slave trade unreservedly was Archbishop Alonso de Montufar of Mexico. Writing to the crown in June 1560, he observed that all the arguments advanced against the enslavement of Amerindians seemed to him to be equally applicable to African Negroes, quite apart from the fact that the Portuguese slave trade itself was riddled with notorious and unchristian abuses. He therefore politely, but ironically, asked King Philip to enlighten him on this problem, and to inform him how the enslavement of black Africans could be justified. Answer came there none; and it is perhaps unlikely that he seriously expected to receive one. In any event, his pertinent query did not find its way into print until over two centuries later.[49]

One singularly forthright condemnation of the West African slave trade and of slavery itself, had in fact appeared in print five years before Montufar penned his reproachful letter. The author, Padre Fernando Oliveira, was a renegade Portuguese Dominican friar, who became an itinerant cleric. In the course of a singularly unconventional and chequered career, he was tutor to the sons of the chronicler João de Barros (1496–1570), author of the first Portuguese grammar (1536) and of a pioneer manual on naval warfare (1555). He was also at one time or another in the service of Henry VIII of England, of Francis I of France, a prisoner of the Moors in Barbary, and in trouble with the Inquisition at Lisbon for his unorthodox and highly original views. In his *Arte da Guerra do Mar* (*Art of Naval Warfare*, 1555), he devoted an entire chapter to a violent denunciation of the Portuguese West African slave trade. He stated flatly that there was no such thing as a "just war" against Muslims, Jews, or pagans who had never been baptized Christians, and who were quite prepared to trade peacefully with the Portuguese. To attack their homelands and to enslave them was a "manifest tyranny," and it was no excuse to say that they indulged in the slave trade with each other. A man who buys something which is wrongfully sold is guilty of sin; and if there were no European buyers, there would be no African sellers. "We were the inventors of such a vile trade, never previously used or heard of among human beings," wrote the indignant padre in a passage which does more credit to his heart than to his head. He scornfully dismissed those merchants who alleged that in buying slaves they were saving souls, retorting that the slave traders were in this sordid business merely for filthy lucre. Not only were the African slaves bought, herded, and treated like cattle, but their children were born and brought up in this degrading servitude even when their parents were baptized Christians, something for which there was no moral justification.[50]

Fernando Oliveira's book was published with the license of the Portuguese Inquisition, but its influence, if any, was minimal. It was never quoted by contemporaries, in so far as I am aware, and obviously it was ignored at Rome. Only one copy of the book seems to be extant at the present day, and its enlightened author was clearly a voice crying in the wilderness.

A wider circulation and consequently better publicity was achieved by one of two contemporary Spanish books, both of which denounced abuses in the Portuguese West African slave trade, although their respective authors did not venture to attack the institution of slavery itself head-on. Fr. Tomás de Mercado, O.P., *Suma de tratos y contratos* (Seville, 1569, 1571, 1573, 1587), and his more outspoken colleague, Fr. Bartolomé de Albornoz, O.P., *Arte de los contractos* (Valencia, 1573), had been in Mexico, and they both denounced the horrors and abuses of the slave trade from personal experience. Albornoz, who was one of the first professors at the University of Mexico, criticized Mercado for not having gone far enough; but though Mercado's book ran through four editions in three decades, Albornoz's work is almost as rare as that of Oliveira. Only two copies appear to be extant at the present day; although I can find no justification for the common assertion that the rarity of the *Arte de los contractos* was due to its being banned by the Inquisition. It does not appear in any of the lists of prohibited books which I have consulted, although another (and unpublished) work of Albornoz does, with which it has been confused by successive bibliographers and historians copying from each other. [51]

During the sixteenth century, the few clerical critics of the slave trade were Dominicans (though Oliveira ended as a secular priest), but in the seventeenth century the Jesuits entered the lists, beginning with Alonso de Sandoval's *Naturaleza, policia sagrada y profana, costumbres y ritos, disciplina y catechismo evangelico de todos Etiopes* (Seville, 1627) [*Nature, sacred and profane policy, customs and rites, evangelical discipline and catechism of all the Ethiopians*]. In this remarkable work, Sandoval (1576–1651), who spent over forty years of his life at the slaving entrepôt of Cartagena de Indias, made a pioneer ethnological survey of the different peoples who were brought as slaves from West Africa to the New World. He also denounced the infamy and horrors of the West African slave trade, particularly as practiced by the Portuguese slave traders, in well-documented and often moving detail. It is true that he did not openly challenge the validity of slavery as an institution, any more than Mercado (whom he frequently quotes) had done.

But the reforms which he suggested should be introduced to regularize the slave trade were so far-reaching that, if implemented, they would in effect have made it quite impracticable, and so resulted in its abandonment or abolition. His work had a second, much revised and altered (but incomplete and not improved) edition in 1647. It does not seem that it had much effect on the practice of the slave trade; although Sandoval inspired the better-known St. Pedro Claver, a Catalan-born Jesuit, in his self-sacrificing endeavors to mitigate its horrors at Cartagena de Indias.[52]

In the 1680s both Charles II, "the bewitched," of Spain, and Pedro II of Portugal had some misgivings about the validity of the West African slave trade; but their scruples of conscience were stiffled by the conviction of their ministers (and perchance of their confessors?) that if this trade was abolished, their respective American empires would no longer be economically viable. An identical attitude was taken by the Jesuit Padre António Vieira (1608–97), the tireless and outspoken champion of the Amerindians in Brazil and the Maranhão. While frankly acknowledging in one of his sermons that very few Negroes from Angola had been legitimately enslaved, he likewise stressed that their blood, sweat and tears nourished and sustained Brazil, which could not dispense with their forced labor under any pretext.[53]

Precisely the same argument, incidentally, was used by Count Johan-Maurits of Nassau-Siegen as the justification for Negro slavery in Netherlands Brazil during his governorship (1637-44). It was also repeated *ad nauseam* by British apologists for the slave trade during the eighteenth century, one of whom characterized Negro slaves as "the strength and sinew of this Western world." Roman Catholics and Protestants alike found ample justification for slavery as an institution in the Old Testament and, to a lesser extent, in the New. Only with the influence of the French Enlightenment, the increasing scruples of the Quakers, and the efforts of late eighteenth century English humanitarians, did the slave trade gradually come under serious, coordinated, and eventually unanswerable attack. But the Vatican's contribution to this gradually changing outlook was precisely nil before the year 1839 — and very little between that date and 1888, when slavery was finally abolished in Brazil.

The Bible, and paricularly the Old Testament, served as an arsenal of texts in support not only of the validity of slavery and of the slave trade but also of color prejudice against the blacks. They were variously alleged to be descended from Cain, who was cursed by God, or from Ham, who was cursed by Noah, and they were doomed accordingly to perpetual bondage. Of course, the defenders of Negroes, like Sandoval, could also quote Scripture for their purpose, instancing the Queen of Sheba and Gaspar, one of the Three Magi, but their arguments made far less impression. Common sense was also occasionally used to combat color prejudice. "Can there be," asked António Vieira rhetorically in his Epiphany Sermon of 1662, "a greater want of understanding, or a greater error of judgement between men as men, than for me to think that I must be your master because I was born further away from the sun, and that you must be my slave because you were born nearer to it?" And again: "An Ethiope if he be cleansed in the waters of the Zaire is clean, but he is not white; but if in the water of baptism he is both." Yet this anticipation of the Protestant poem, "And I am black, but Oh! my soul is white" did not prevent Vieira from arguing to the end of his days, as had Las Casas for most of his long life, that the freedom of the Amerindians could best be secured by increasing the importation of Negro slaves from West Africa. Just as the undeniable fact that Christ's mother, the Virgin Mary, was a Jewess, did little or nothing to stem the tide of antisemitism in Christian Europe for centuries, so black people of both sexes were basically regarded as essentially inferior, or often as subhuman, even if one or two of them were popularly believed to have been saints.

It is often alleged that religious orders, and more particularly the Jesuits, treated their slaves relatively well, certainly better than did the average layman. I have this impression myself; but we need much more research in this field before adequate statistical proof is forthcoming in one way or the other. In any event, the church also acted as a medium of social control over the slaves; just as it did with the poor and the working classes of Europe, where both Catholic priests and Protestant ministers usually inculcated the virtues of obedience and respect to social superiors — "God bless the squire and his relations, and keep us in our proper stations."[54] As Nicholas Cushner, S. J. has written in a recent article: "The Spanish version of Roman Catholicism, particularly among the Jesuits, was especially sensitive to hierarchical obedience. The slaves were taught that their state was ordained by God Himself, that their only duty was to obey their masters, and that their reward for this would come in heaven."[55] This was certainly the burden of António Vieira's sermons addressed to the slaves, when he compared their sufferings in the sugar mills at harvest time, working round the clock, to those of Christ upon the Cross. Urging them to bear their lot with the same fortitude and resignation, he assured them that they would be suitably recompensed in Paradise. In other words: "Work and pray, live on hay, you'll get pie in the sky when you die."

From this survey it is evident that the champions of the Church Militant were usually very reluctant to share their sacerdotal status with any non-European peoples, even when the latter had been Christians for several generations. Even where race prejudice did not make itself felt in the first contacts of Europeans with colored peoples overseas, it invariably did so with the passage of time to a greater or lesser extent. Biblical authority, Aristotelian (or pseudo-Aristotelian) theories of natural racial superiority and inferiority, reinforced the innate conviction of Christians in general and of militant missionaries in particular, that "The faith is Europe and Europe is the Faith," as Hilaire Belloc is alleged to have maintained. Their conviction of moral and intellectual superiority, which is further exemplified in the next chapter, was reinforced by the increasing stress laid in the Iberian peninsula on "purity of blood" (*limpeza de sangue* in Portuguese, *limpieza de sangre* in Spanish) as an essential requirement for any municipal or ecclesiastical office. Originally intended as a religious and racial bar against persons of "Moorish" (i.e., Muslim) and Jewish origins, it was swiftly extended to include African blacks, owing to their association with chattel slavery, and in due course to most other non-Europeans as well. Persons of mixed blood were usually regarded with suspicion, dislike, and disdain, due to the erroneous belief that the colored blood [*sic*] contaminated the white, as the history of *mesticos* in the Portuguese empire and of mestizos in the Spanish empire shows. There were exceptions in all times and in all places. But both Iberian empires remained essentially a "pigmentocracy" (to use Magnus Morner's expression), based on the conviction of white racial, moral, and intellectual superiority—just as did their Dutch, English, and French successors.

CHAPTER TWO

Cultural Interactions

As Peter Gay has observed in his stimulating and standard work on the Enlightenment: "Even the most genial Christian had to regard his religion as absolutely true (and therefore all others as radically false) and heathens as unwitting precursors, or unregenerate enemies, or miserable souls in need of light."[1] This conviction, held by a great majority of Europeans for centuries, was inevitably still more firmly embedded in the missionaries who went overseas to convert the "benighted heathen." Whether these latter-day apostles were sixteenth-century Iberian priests and friars or nineteenth-century Protestant evangelists, they were certain that they possessed the sole key to salvation in this world and the next. The deeply rooted conviction that their religion alone represented "the Way, the Truth, the Life," and that all other creeds were either inherently false or else sadly distorted, was inevitably the bedrock belief of any individual with a missionary vocation.

I do not know who coined the adage: "One man's belief is another man's superstition"; but this Voltairean-sounding sentiment can hardly have originated with a missionary. European missionaries were, by and large, predisposed to consider themselves the bearers not merely of a superior religion but of a superior culture, the two being so inseparably intertwined. Admittedly, some missionaries modified their views in this respect after greater experience of the mission-field. But the basic conviction of religious and cultural superiority stayed with most of them to the end; otherwise they would hardly have

remained missionaries. Convinced as they were of the moral—
and usually of the material—superiority of Western Christendom, only the exceptional missionary took the time and the
trouble deeply to study the sacred books (where such existed)
and the basic beliefs of those whom they were trying to convert,
as did, for example, Sahagún in Mexico, Ricci in China, and
Nobili in India. Most of the sowers of the Gospel seed were
inclined to dismiss such beliefs as the work of the Devil, and all
non-Christian cultures as either basically inferior or oddly
exotic. Moreover, Iberian missionaries came from a cultural
background which did not predispose them to manifest much
intellectual curiosity about the "many and jarring peoples"
(*muita e desvairada gente*) with whom they came into contact.
As one of the leading authorities, Padre António da Silva Rego,
commented a few years ago when the collapse of the Portuguese
colonial empire was not foreseen: "Although race relations
always produce an exchange of culture—what is now known as
acculturation—the Portuguese in my opinion, were unconscious
receivers and conscious givers. That is: they were not consciously prepared to receive anything, or to adapt themselves to
local conditions and environment; on the contrary, they were
consciously convinced of the superiority of their culture and of
their way of life. [2]

Obviously, there were many exceptions, such as the Portuguese settlers in the hinterland of Angola and in Zambesia, who
became increasingly Africanized in the course of time. But this
development was not the result of official policy, but in spite of
it, due to the lack of white women. It did not affect the
missionaries of the Church Militant to the same extent, for
obvious reasons. Since the interactions between Christian and
non-Christian cultures in the zones of Iberian domination or of
Iberian influence were so varied, we can only briefly consider a
few aspects thereof. Let us begin by taking a rapid survey of the
printing press as a medium of Christian propaganda by the
Church Militant in the non-Christian world; and then glance
successively at varying missionary attitudes to the religions and
cultures of Africa, America, and Asia.

THE PRINTED WORD AND THE SPREAD OF THE FAITH

The great bulk of the works produced by printing presses, whether clerical or lay, for the use of missionaries in the field, can be divided into the following main categories: (a) catechisms and other compendia of the basic tenets of Christianity; (b) linguistics, including grammars, dictionaries, and vocabularies; (c) manuals and guides for the use of confessors and parish priests; (d) edifying, apologetical, and polemical works.

Compendia of the basic tenets of Christianity, usually entitled *Doctrina Christiana*, or similar, translated into the respective vernaculars, were obviously of primary importance to the missionaries wherever they labored. It is just possible that one was printed for use in the old kingdom of Congo by the two German printers who are recorded as having left Lisbon for West Africa in 1492; but, if so, we have no record of it. However, the first book printed in a Bantu language was a bilingual *Doctrina Christiana*, with Portuguese and Ki-Kongo in interlinear text, published at Lisbon in 1624, for the use of missionaries in Congo and Angola.[3] The first printed catechism on the other side of the Atlantic was a brief one in Spanish and Nahuatl, published at Mexico City in 1539—exactly a century before the first book came off the press in New England. This pioneer *Doctrina* was followed by a host of others compiled in the principal languages of New Spain and Guatemala during the remainder of the colonial period. The press in South America was rather later off the mark and never so productive as in Mexico; but a *Doctrina* printed in Spanish, Quechua, and Aymará (Lima, 1584) was the second book printed in Peru, and the forerunner of many other such works in the indigenous languages of that vast viceroyalty.[4]

In 1554 a catechism in romanized Tamil and in Portuguese was published at Lisbon for the benefit of some leading converts who had just arrived from the Fishery Coast of Southwest India.[5] Three years later, a *Doctrina* by St. Francis Xavier, in Portuguese only, was published by the Jesuit press at Goa, which had been established there the year before (1556), although no extant copy is known. This was the first of many Jesuit *Doctrinas* published around the world, literally from China to Peru. It was based upon that of the famous chronicler, João de Barros (c. 1496–1570), which had been printed at Lisbon in 1539. Next come the catechisms in Tamil characters printed in 1578 and 1579, respectively, one copy of each edition having survived. The former is the earliest known example of a catechism in an indigenous script, as distinct from a romanized version.[6] In 1584 a catechism in Chinese characters was published at Chao Ch'ing in a block-printed (xylographic) edition. The same method was used for the pioneer *Doctrinas* in Spanish and Tagalog, and in Spanish and Chinese, both published at Manila in 1593, one copy of each having survived.[7] Turning to Japan, we find that among the earliest productions of the celebrated Jesuit mission-press which flourished there from 1590 to 1613, were catechisms in romanized Japanese (*romaji*) and in Japanese script, printed in 1591–92.[8]

These catechisms vary in length from a few pages to more than a hundred, one of the more substantial being that in the language of the Kariri Indians in Brazil, published by a French Franciscan missionary at Lisbon in 1709.[9] Finally, we may note that these Roman Catholic catechisms provided the precedent for the pioneer production of the Danish Lutheran mission-press established at Tranquebar on the Coromandel Coast of India in 1712. This book was a Protestant *Doctrina*, in which the languages employed were Portuguese and Tamil, just as they had been in the Jesuit *Doctrinas* published on the opposite (Malabar) Coast. The press itself had been supplied by the Society for Promoting Christian Knowledge at London.

The linguistic works published by or for the missionaries were equally far-ranging. Among the more innovative may be mentioned pioneer grammars in Nahuatl (*Arte de la lengua Mexicana*, 1571); Aymara (1612); Guaraní (Madrid, 1640, and Puebla de Santa Maria la Mayor, Paraguay, 1724); Konkani (1640); Tagalog (1610); Chinese (1703); and Japanese (1604–8). There was also a wide range of dictionaries, beginning with one in

Nahuatl by Fr. Alonso de Medina, O.F.M. (1555), and including a Tamil-Portuguese vocabulary printed by the Jesuits at Ambalacat (Kerala) in 1679.[10] These works which achieved the dignity of print, often after years of intensive effort in compiling them, were supplemented by many copies which circulated in manuscript, as did others which never got into print.

This is an aspect of missionary activity which was and is deserving of the highest praise. Such works were of course undertaken, ''for the greater glory of God,'' but they are of the greatest value and interest for lexicographers and language students at the present day. The study of the Portuguese Jesuit João Rodrigues's Japanese grammars of 1604–8 and 1620 (this last printed at Macao) is almost a minor industry among Japanese scholars who are researching and publishing on the history of their own language.[11] On the other side of the world, nineteenth- and twentieth-century efforts to reconstruct the basic language of the extinct Tupí tribes of Brazil, take as their starting point the pioneer grammar compiled by the Jesuit missionary José de Anchieta (*Arte de Grammatica de Lingoa mais usada na costa do Brasil* [Coimbra, 1595]). In addition to the foregoing works and many others like them, which were published in the mission-field with which they were concerned, or in the Iberian peninsula, a valuable series of grammars and vocabularies of the worldwide scope was also produced by the presses of the Congregation of the Propaganda Fide, established at Rome in 1622. Even the suppression of the Society of Jesus in 1759–73, involving the dispersion, imprisonment, and death of its members, did not stop the flow of Jesuit publications in this field, as instanced by the works of some of the exiled Jesuits in Italy. It will suffice to recall here, Padre Lorenzo Hervás y Panduro (1735–1809), and his pioneer works on comparative philology.[12]

The manuals, guides, and handbooks published for the use of confessors and parish priests form another important and valuable category. Although the religious orders rightly placed great stress on the need for the missionary in any particular

field to learn the language involved, there was often a time lag
before a confessor could hear a penitent in his own tongue. He
had perforce to resort to an interpreter and/or a *confessionario*.
These latter contained the questions to be asked, as well as
likely responses, together with their Spanish or Portuguese
translations. Such handbooks were probably more numerous in
manuscript versions than in printed copies, but many of the
latter have survived. A notable pioneer of this category was Fr.
Alonso de Molina, O.F.M. (c. 1513–85) whose *Confessionario
breve en lengua mexicana*, first published at Mexico in 1563/64
had numerous later editions. The interest and importance of
these *confessionarios* for social historians and for anthropolo-
gists has only recently been realized. One of the few scholars to
utilize them is Dr. Francisco Guerra, M.D., who has exploited
them in connection with the study of Amerindian sexual practices and hallucinatory drugs in his *The Pre-Columbian Mind*
(1971).

If the study of *Confessionarios*, literally (again!) from China
to Peru, will tell us something about the beliefs and the
psychology of converts to Christianity, the *Guides* for parish
priests are equally illuminating for the interaction between
Iberian and overseas cultures. One of the most interesting is the
previously mentioned *Itinerario para Parochos de Indios*
(Madrid, 1668), by Fr. Alonso de la Peña Montenegro. His experience was mainly in South America; and for the viceroyalty of
Mexico we have (among others) the *Indian Lantern,* or *Farol in-
diano y guía de curas de Indios* (Mexico, 1713), a delightful work
in Spanish and Nahuatl by Manual Perez, who held a professor-
ship in this latter language for about twenty-two years.[13] On the
farthest extremity of the Spanish empire, we may instance the
Parocho de Indios instruido (Manila, 1745) by one of the most
active Spanish missionary-friars in the Philippines. It is a work
of lasting value for the social history of that time and country.[14]
Edifying, apologetical, and polemical works produced by Iberian
missionaries in the field, whether manuscript or printed, were
likewise extremely numerous and were directed at friends and

foes on all fronts. Lives of Saints (*Flos Sanctorum*) were published in many languages and in many versions, including a magnificent Tamil edition, of which only one copy survives, in 1587. Lives of the Virgin were naturally in demand, including one published at Goa in 1652, of which seven or eight copies survive. The publications of the relatively short lived but fascinating Jesuit press in Japan (1592–1613), include translations or adaptations of edifying works by St. Ignatius Loyola (1596), Fr. Bartholomeu dos Martires (1596) and Fr. Luís de Granada (1592, 1599, 1611), to mention only those by contemporary Iberian authors. The tally was naturally much longer in countries where the mission-presses were able to function continuously, such as in Spanish America and the Philippines, or even, for that matter, in China.[15] Polemical works formed a much smaller category, for obvious reasons, but a passing mention may be made of two which were published at Goa. The Archbishop of Goa published an anti-Jewish tract in 1565, accompanied by an exhortation addressed to "the people of Israel, still following the Law of Moses and of the Talmud, through the error and malice of their Rabbis."[16] Nearly eighty years later (1642) the Jesuit press at Goa published a violent diatribe against the Ethiopian Coptic church, printed in Abyssinian type with Latin translation.[17] Since the Jesuit missionaries in the quondam realm of Prester John had been killed or driven out in the previous decade, and that country remained closed to Western Christianity for some two centuries, it is unlikely that this last work ever reached those for whom it was intended.

THE CHURCH MILITANT
AND AFRICAN AND AMERINDIAN CULTURES

Turning to consider briefly some of the reactions of the missionaries of the Church Militant to the cultures and civilizations which they successively encountered overseas, from tropical Africa to the snows of Tibet, we find something like the following. By the early seventeenth century, when Iberian expansion in most regions had reached its apogee, the Western intruders were inclinded to rate the Asian cultures as the highest, though still below the level of occidental Christendom; the major American civilizations (Aztec, Inca, Maya) as next best; and Black Africans jostling for the bottom position with the Caribs, the Tupí, and the other untamed "savages" of the New World. Such, in essence, was the classification of civilizations and cultures proposed by Padre José de Acosta, S.J., although he was careful to add that there was great variety and many subdivisions within those three main categories. His view was certainly shared by the majority of missionaries who worked in Africa, and who were wont to contrast unfavorably the half-civilized, or the uncivilized Bantu (as they saw them) with the highly civilized Japanese and Chinese.

Nevertheless, there were some people who took a relatively favorable view of the Bantu potential, including several of the Jesuits in Angola. At one time, they reported optimistically: "The heathen of Angola are one of the most suitable people in Africa and Guinea to receive our Holy Faith, for they are very intelligent, although those Europeans who do not understand their language regard them as clowns (boçais), as for that matter they regard us when they cannot understand our language. This is the reason why our Fathers try very hard to learn their language; because if we do so, we can get along with them, and there will be no difficulty about converting them all to Christianity." [18] Similarly, a Jesuit Padre of considerable experience in Zambesia, recalled how he had witnessed a group of Bantu listening to a Portuguese fidalgo strumming away on his guitar, and had overheard one of the black bystanders observe to his companions: "You see, these savages have musical instruments just like we do." The Jesuit translated this remark for the benefit of his compatriots, who were much amused thereat. [19] But there is no reason to suppose that it shook their basic conviction that Negros boçais were best fitted for the conversion of their immortal souls and the enslavement of their vile bodies.

Missionary reactions to the major Amerindian civilizations were more positive, at any rate in some respects. We have no work on the Bantu, or on the Sudanese peoples of Guinea, to compare with the writings of Bartolomé de Las Casas, O.P., Bernardino de Sahagun, O.F.M., José de Acosta, S.J., and Diego de Landa, O.F.M., on various Amerindian cultures, to name only a few of the most obvious names in this connection. Work on Las Casas has become a minor (or a major?) historical industry since Lewis Hanke opened up this rich vein to a wider public nearly half a century ago. [20] Sahagún's work is now available in truly monumental form, [21] but Diego de Landa is less well-known, so a few words on him may not be amiss.

A Franciscan missionary-friar in Yucatán from 1549 to 1563, and bishop of that diocese from 1572 until his death there in 1579, he achieved a somewhat dubious celebrity for his zeal in ferreting out and hunting down idolatrous practices among the Maya, often extracting confessions by means of torture. He was also responsible for consigning to the flames many of the Maya writings, or "codices" as they are now styled, recording the indigenous customs and beliefs. But he likewise compiled an *Account of the Affairs of Yucatán (Relación de las cosas de Yucatán)* about 1566, which his latest editor describes as being the most detailed account of the ancient Maya to have survived from the early colonial period, when some contact with the pre-Hispanic past was still possible and the processes of cultural dissolution were not yet far advanced.

The *Relación* was probably intended for the instruction of future missionaries. The methods of inquiry which he used were similar to those employed by Sahagún in Mexico, although he did not attain his colleague's depth of insight and objectivity. Essentially, his approach consisted of collecting written testimonials, oral accounts, and the replies of witnesses to a number of set questions. He used a wide variety of informants including several pioneer *conquistadores*, various native chieftains, and representatives of the leading Xiu, Cocom, and Chel families. The result, despite its inevitable missionary bias of "one man's religion is another man's superstition," is the only contemporary account which we have of the customs, social organization, and beliefs of the Maya at the time of the conquest.[22] It also reflected Landa's conviction that in order to convert an individual it was first necessary to understand his (or her) beliefs — a glimpse of the obvious today, but which was not widely spread among Europeans in the sixteenth century.

The fascinating work of the Jesuit missionary José de Acosta on the *Natural and Moral History of the Indies* (*Historia Natural y Moral de las Indias*) published at Seville in 1590, was a bestseller in its own day and generation, and it has deservedly remained a classic ever since. It elicited the unstinted praise of Alexander von Humboldt as a masterpiece on physical geography. In this and in several of his other works, Acosta shows a balanced appreciation of the great Amerindian civilizations in general and of the Incas in particular. His wide-ranging curiosity enabled him to take a global view of many cultural and ethnographical problems which had hitherto been treated in isolation. His works can still be consulted with pleasure and profit.[23]

While most of the studies on indigenous beliefs and customs were undertaken by missionaries, there were some other individuals who made important contributions toward the understanding of the American past and the cultural changes wrought by the Spanish conquest. Alonso de Zurita, successively *Oidor* (High Court Judge) of Santo Domingo, Guatemala, and Mexico (1547–65), wrote an impassioned criticism of the mistreatment of the Amerindians by their new masters which recalls the vehement denunciations of Las Casas. But his *Brief Account of the Lords of New Spain*, compiled c. 1590, did not achieve the same fame and notoriety, remaining unpublished until the twentieth century.[24]

In contrast to Zurita, who was unreservedly pro-Amerindian, a much more ambivalent attitude was taken by the celebrated Mexican Creole scholar, Don Carlos de Sigüenza y Gongora (1645–1700). Expelled from the Society of Jesus for moral turpitude when still a novice, he became a secular priest, mathematician, astronomer, historian, antiquarian, poet, and critic. He was professor of mathematics at Mexico University, Cosmographer-Royal to Charles, "the bewitched," and he politely rejected an invitation by Louis XIV to become a pensioner at the court of Versailles. He spent years studying the pre-Conquest history of Mexico, collecting many codices and artifacts in the process, including the works of the mestizo chronicler Fernando de Alva Ixtlilxochital (1568–1648). The proletarian riot at Mexico City in June 1692, of which he was a horrified eyewitness, brought about an abrupt shift in his attitude toward the Amerindians. Wereas he had previously been rather sympathetic to their plight, he thenceforth denounced them as "the most ungrateful, ignorant, whining and restless people that God ever created, the most favoured with privileges [by the Crown] under whose protection they basely commit crimes and misdeeds."[25]

THE CHURCH MILITANT AND ASIAN CULTURES

India

If we compare the situation in Portuguese Asia with that in Spanish America during the first half of the sixteenth century, we find that the Portuguese missionaries were much slower in seriously studying the beliefs and the cultures of those whom they were trying to convert than were their Spanish colleagues in New Spain and Peru. Until the Jesuits arrived with new men and new methods at Goa in 1542, relatively few missionaries had been sent out from Portugal and they had achieved relatively little. Most of them were Franciscan friars, but they provided no counterparts to the famous "Twelve Apostles," headed by Fr. Martin de Valencia, O.F.M., who had done so much for the spiritual conquest of Mexico from 1524 onward.[26] As indicated above, neither the pioneer friars nor the secular clergy in Asia for a long time took the trouble to study the

sacred books and the basic religious beliefs of their potential
converts, whether Muslim, Hindu, or Buddhist, being inclined
to dismiss them all out of hand as the works of the Devil.
Exceptions there were, but they were few and far between.
They included an (unidentified) friar, who told the Inquisitors at
Goa in 1620 that he had made careful study of Hinduism in all
the places where he had been, not only because of his need to do
so as a missionary, but because he was naturally inquisitive and
a seeker after knowledge. [27]

The first recorded attempt to make use of the sacred Hindu
books is narrated in a letter written by Pedro de Almeida, S.J.,
at Goa on the 26 December 1558. He relates how the Jesuits had
found in the house of a prominent Hindu, a long religious poem
entitled *Anadí-Purana,* "in which are written most of their
falsities and fables of their gods. We are having these translated
so that we can learn about their blind fancies. In the small
portion that has been done hitherto, we have the narrative of
the origin and creation of their gods, and how they came to this
world in diverse forms, such as tortoise, pig, fish, hyacinth, and
other absurdities. It also describes the different kinds of gods
and their names," including Rama, Govinda, and Ganesh. "In
the portion which remains to be translated, we hope to discover
many falsities, which will help us to confound those who believe
in them. The man who owned this bible was seized, . . . and as
a punishment for him and his like, and in order to favor
christianity, he was paraded in a halter in the public squares of
the city and sentenced to a chain-gang for four months." [28]

The English Jesuit Thomas Stevens, who worked in Portuguese India for forty years (1579–1619), became very fluent in
Marathí, composing a Christian *Purana,* which was published at
Rachol in 1616. Written in the style of the Hindu *Puranas,* but
printed in romanized Marathí, and entitled (in translation)
Discourse of the coming of our Savior Jesus Christ to the World,
it became a classic in the literature of the vernacular, and very
popular with the local Christian communities. Manuscript copies
continued to circulate until into the twentieth century. Stevens's
method was followed by a French Jesuit, alias Estevão da Cruz,

who wrote a *Purana* in Marathi-Konkani on the life of St. Peter, which was published at Goa in 1634. [29]

In addition to these two Christian *puranas* which achieved the dignity of print, there were similar works which circulated only in manuscript or in oral tradition. One example will suffice. In 1626, Fr. António Peixoto, a Franciscan missionary, in Ceylon staged a play (*comedia*) in Sinhalese verse, which he had written himself for the edification of the faithful on the martyrdom of St. John the Baptist. ''The work was performed with great splendour and at night, for these people are wont to have their theatrical performances by night. This play was very well attended, not only by all the local Christians, but by the heathen, as they are very keen to attend such performances which they greatly enjoy, much appreciating the poetry, which they hold in high esteem.''[30]

The attempt of the Italian Jesuit Robert de' Nobili (1577–1656) to convert the Brahmins of Madura by assimilating their customs and behavior as far as was consistent with the profession of Christianity, was regarded dubiously by most of his Portuguese colleagues, although he had some supporters.[31] Nobili's fame has eclipsed the work of a Portuguese Jesuit, Sebastião Gonçalves (1561–1640), author of a *History of Malabar,* compiled in 1615 but first published 340 years later. Despite its title, it is not so much a history of Malabar as a handbook for Jesuit missionaries, describing clearly and succinctly the religion, manners, customs and traditions, of the coastal region of Southwest India. It contains one of the earliest European outlines of Hinduism, with a section devoted to a refutation of Hindu beliefs, contrasting them with Roman Catholicism as the only true religion. The author's antipathy to Hinduism makes this polemical part of no great value; but the earlier chapters, describing the country, the caste system and the people as they were in 1615, are particularly interesting for Travancore and the adjoining Dravidian-speaking coastal districts.[32]

A much more detailed treatise on Hinduism by another Portuguese Jesuit, Gonçalo Fernandes Trancoso, (c. 1521–1621), was compiled in the Madura mission in 1616, but it lay unread in the Jesuit archives at Rome until published by Fr. Josef Wicki, S.J., in 1973.[33] Neither Gonçalves nor Fernandes knew Sanskrit; but they derived their information from Tamil and Malayalam intermediaries. The same qualification applies to Francisco Garcia (158?- 1659), who was archbishop of Cranganore from 1641 until his death. He has not had a very good press from modern ecclesiastical historians, owing to his controversial attitude to the St. Thomas Christians of Malabar. But he seems to have been the first European to translate directly from the vernacular some Indian folklore and fables, which only became known in the West over a century and a half later. Among them was the perenially popular tale of King Vikrama's adventures, *The Thirty-two Tales of the Throne*, which Garcia translated from a Marathi version.[34]

I need hardly add that even those Portuguese missionaries who studied Hinduism and Indian culture seriously, if not exactly sympathetically, never lost their basic Eurocentric viewpoint, nor their patriotic pride in Portugal as the *Alferes da Fé*, the Ensign or Standard-bearer of the Faith. Typical in this respect was Padre Fernão de Queiroz, S.J. (1617-88). He is best known today as the author of a massive if ill-digested work on the Portuguese in Sri Lanka, *Temporal and Spiritual Conquest of Ceylon* (1687), which for all its faults of prolixity and presentation, is still a prime source for the period with which it deals. Queiroz was also the author of a curious mystical and messianic book, *History of the Life of the Venerable Brother Pedro de Basto* (1689), as mentioned in Chapter four below.

A lifetime spent in India did not change the ardent missionary's Eurocentric outlook. He did inculcate the importance of learning one or more of the Indian vernaculars, and he did criticize many of his colleagues for their failure to distinguish between Hinduism and Buddhism. But he sweepingly dismissed all Asian languages as "barbarous," though admitting that some of their poetry sounded well enough. He added that the contents of Oriental prose and verse could not measure up to European standards, with the partial exception of the Chinese literature. "But incredible is the energy which Asians display in their poetry, in which they declaim their *Vedas*, and their *Puranas*, which means their scriptures and the doctrines of their sciences, such as these are. But as, with the exception of China, they have achieved perfection in no faculty, neither their prose nor their poetry can be compared with Greek and Latin works, or with modern European ones."[35]

China

Fernão de Queiroz's rather grudging admission that Chinese civilization and culture might be comparable to those of Europe, save for lack of the only true revealed religion, reflects a widely accepted Western generalization. It goes back to the Portuguese chronicler, João de Barros, writing his *Decade I* in 1539, but published in 1552, the year of St. Francis Xavier's death on an offshore island in the South China Sea. The Chinese returned the compliment after a fashion, saying that they had two eyes, the Europeans one, and all the rest of mankind were blind.[36] Although schemes for the conquest and conversion of China were seriously discussed at Manila and Malacca during the last quarter of the sixteenth century, these fantastic projects were never countenanced by the responsible authorities at Goa, Lisbon, Mexico City, and Madrid. They are of interest only as showing the persistence of the Iberian *conquistador* mentality and the missionary zeal of the Church Militant with which it was so closely intertwined.[37]

European fascination with China and the sustained interest of the reading public — or a substantial portion thereof — in Chinese government, civilization and culture, was largely the work of missionary writers who (after about 1600) could and did circulate throughout the Middle Flowery Kingdom; whereas European merchants and mariners were confined to a few seaports, of which Macao and Canton were the chief. One of the outstanding bestsellers of the sixteenth century was Juan González de Mendoza's *Historia de las cosas más notables, ritos y costumbres del gran Reyno de la China*, first printed at Rome in 1585.

By the end of the century, thirty editions of this book had been published in the principal European languages. Mendoza himself was never in China, but his book (compiled in Mexico) is a skillful synthesis of earlier accounts by Portuguese and Spaniards. His chief sources were the 1569 *Tractado* of the Portuguese Dominican friar, Gaspar da Cruz, and the *Relacíon* (1575) of the Spanish Augustinian friar, Martín de Rada. As G. F. Hudson has observed: "Mendoza's book reaches the very essentials of the life of Old China, and its publication may be taken to mark the date from which an adequate knowledge of China was available for the learned world of Europe."[38] But it did more than this. For the better educated section of the European reading public, China now became an enviable country, where justice was well administered, where the people were contented and hard working, peaceable and self-controlled. Only in the all-important matter of revealed religion did the Chinese fall short of the highest achievement of the West; but God would doubtless remedy this defect in due time.

Throughout the seventeenth century, a steady stream of books on China continued to meet the equally steady demand. Most of them were by Jesuit missionaries, beginning with Matteo Ricci's account as filtered through the Belgian Jesuit Nicholas Trigault's *De Christiana Expeditione apud Sinas* (Augsburg, 1615), and ending with the French Jesuit Louis Le Comte's *Nouveaux Memoires sur l'Etat present de la Chine* (Paris, 1696). The China craze reached a crescendo in the eighteenth century with the publication of the French series of the *Lettres Edifiantes et Curieuses* (1702–76) and its Austro-German counterpart, the *Welt Bott* (1726–61). These serial publications contained information on other missions, including those in India and Hispanic America, but it was the Chinese material which provided the chief interest. Although the bulk of Europe's knowledge on China was derived from French sources, there were some influential Iberian contributions, better known perhaps in foreign editions or versions than in their respective homelands. Among them were the Spanish Dominican, Domingo

Fernández de Navarrete's *Tratados de la Gran China* (1676, 1679), and the Portuguese Jesuit Gabriel de Magalhães's *Doze Excellencias da China* (1688).[39]

An aspect of these and similar works which is sometimes overlooked, is that the European editors often took considerable liberties with the originals, either toning down or else (more rarely) adding criticism of the Chinese. For example, a perusal of Fr. Martín de Rada's original narrative of his short but productive visit to Fukien in 1575, reveals that he was a good deal more critical of Chinese culture than his Mexican-based editor, González de Mendoza, implied in his widely read *Historia* (1585). Although Rada took care to assemble a representative collection of Chinese books, which he brought back with him to Manila, he scornfully dismissed most of them as containing only the name and smell (*olor*) of the subjects with which they dealt. He was very contemptuous of Chinese achievements in astronomy, mathematics, and the natural sciences. He made an exception for Chinese herbals, which he found were as well-illustrated as the contemporary European editions of Dioscorides. He even went so far as to rate the knowledge of the Chinese in some respects as not much higher than that of the half savage (in his view) Filipinos. González de Mendoza either omitted or toned down most of Rada's asperities in his *Historia* of 1585, following the more favorable line of his Portuguese predecessor, Gaspar da Cruz, O.P., in his *Tratado* of 1569.[40]

I may add that some of the eighteenth-century French Jesuit missionaries in China complained of the way in which their Parisian editor, Père Jean Baptiste du Halde (1674–1743) handled the material which they sent him, or to which he had access. These critics included Père Antoine Gaubil (1689–1759) probably the most accomplished Sinologue of the eighteenth century. It was obviously difficult for Du Halde, who had never been in China, accurately to evaluate all the information he received, and to edit it in a form which would edify the piety as well as tickle the curiosity of his readers. Du Halde also had to cope with the lucubrations of the Jesuit 'Figurists', who tried to find in the Chinese classics veiled allusions to and confirmatory evidence of Old Testament traditions. Perhaps we may leave the last word to Antoine Gaubil, who wrote from Peking to the secretary of the Royal Society at London in 1753: "I . . . hope that Mr. Costard and many other gentlemen in England, France, and elsewhere, will lay aside their doubts or prejudices about Chinese astronomy and antiquities. It is, indeed really difficult to take the just medium between those who too highly extoll and those who unduly despise Chinese literature."[41]

Japan

We have seen that the fertile imagination of some Iberian *conquistadores* and stalwarts of the Church Militant led them in all seriousness to propose the conquest of China in the late sixteenth century, but no such proposal was ever made to subdue their more warlike neighbors, the Japanese. On the contrary, the Europeans soon learned to be careful how they handled this formidable race. The first recorded armed clash resulted in the deaths of several Portuguese in 1561. Jan Huighen van Linschoten, admittedly no great admirer of the Portuguese, commented on this affair some thirty-five years later: "I think it happened by their filthy pride and presumptuousness, for in all places they will be lords and masters, to the contempt and embasing of the inhabitants, which in all places will not be endured, namely in Japan, they being a stubborn and obstinate people."[42] Even if Linschoten was mistaken in this particular instance, it cannot be denied that "pride and presumptuousness" characterized the behavior of many Europeans in Asia from the days of Vasco da Gama to the Western débacle at the beginning of World War II. But the martial qualities of the Japanese ensured that neither the Iberian *conquistadores*, nor their Dutch and English successors, treated them as cavalierly as they did the Indians, the Indonesians, or the Chinese.

The Jesuit and other missionaries who worked and traveled in Japan during the period 1549–1614 had one great advantage over the Protestant Dutch traders who were the only Europeans allowed in the island empire between 1640 and 1852. They knew the language, whereas the Netherlanders, Germans, Scandinavians, and other employees of the Dutch East India Company "of laudable and redoubtable name," who were cooped up in Nagasaki, were forbidden to learn Japanese and were compelled to rely on indigenous interpreters. The reports of the missionaries, and more particularly of the Jesuits, who were the pioneers in Japan and far more numerous than their friar colleagues and rivals, have long been recognized as primary sources for the study of Japanese history in one of its crucial periods. Their letters from the mission-field, sometimes drastically edited, achieved quite a wide circulation in Europe, 1550–1640, though they did not arouse the same interest as was manifested later in those from China.[43] Still we may note that 1,000 copies of a Spanish edition of Jesuit letters from Japan were printed at Alcalá in 1575, and were distributed free of charge.

The best and most perceptive Jesuit account of Japan was the work of the Portuguese Padre João Rodrigues (c. 1561–1633), nicknamed Tçuzzu, or "interpreter," on account of his exceptional knowledge of the language. It was left unfinished at his death, and has only recently been made available in a satisfactory form. Unlike most of his colleagues and compatriots, Rodrigues was not merely familiar with the external facts of Japanese culture, but he displayed a remarkable appreciation of the underlying values and aesthetics of the indigenous art and literature. His analytical accounts of many aspects of Japanese life, including etiquette, festivals, and architecture, are distinguished for their meticulous detail. His exceptional grasp of the complicated rituals of the tea ceremony has impressed present-day practitioners. He had a singularly sensitive appreciation of Japanese poetry, on which he wrote a masterly introductory essay in his Japanese *Grammar* of 1604–8. This was the first comprehensive description of a branch of Far Eastern literature by any European; and it was not surpassed in its own field until

Satow and Chamberlain took up this topic in the last quarter of the nineteenth century. [44]

Rodrigues's work, though smaller in volume, stands comparison with those of Sahagún and Motolinia on Aztec Mexico. Unfortunately, it had even less influence. His massive *História* remained unfinished and unpublished. His *Arte* or *Grammar* of 1604–8 was read only by a few missionaries, arousing no interest worth mentioning until modern times. There are only two known copies of this fascinating work; and so far as most of his compatriots in the Far East were concerned, it might as well have remained unwritten. In the same year that Rodrigues died at Macao, the governor, who must have known him quite well, referred to the Japanese authorities at Nagasaki as "these Niggers" in his official correspondence with Goa. [45]

In Japan, as elsewhere, the Jesuit missionaries encouraged their converts to stage theatrical representations (*autos*) of a religious nature, particularly on major feast days, such as Christmas, Easter, and the Day of Kings (6 January). Japanese converts took these *autos* with enthusiasm, if the Jesuit descriptions of them can be taken at face value. Quite elaborate scenes were staged, accompanied by both European and Japanese music. An eyewitness description of an Easter procession in 1562, reads in part:"In that procession of the Resurrection, several incidents in Holy Scripture were represented, such as the flight of the children of Israel from Egypt, for which purpose a Red Sea was made, which opened to let the Israelites pass and then closed again when Pharaoh was passing with his army. The story of the Prophet Jonas was also depicted, showing him coming out of the whale, and other such stories. When the procession was over, the people were exhorted to contrast the sadness of the Passion with the joy of the Resurrection." [46]

The night of Christmas Eve was celebrated with special fervor, and the following extract from the same letter can be regarded as typical. "Before showing the birth of Christ, they acted the flooding of the world in the time of Noah, and his entry into the Ark. This was followed by the captivity of Lot and the victory of Abraham. All these scenes were so well mounted and presented, that it did not look as if they were being acted but were real. . . . Finally came the arrival of the shepherds to the crib." On such occasions, the churches were thronged, with the men being on one side and the women on the other, as in Portugal. In the intervals between the scenes, or even during them, the congregation chanted "verses narrating the whole life of Our Lord, extolling His Glory, His holy name and His holy cross, and the Christian religion. Other verses denounced the blindness of the heathen and the deceit of the devil. And in this way they spent nearly the whole night long, singing everything in their own language, whereby the Padre was greatly edified." Some of these religious plays also featured a chorus, who commented on the action in moralizing fashion, like the role of the chorus in a Greek tragedy.[47]

The prohibition of Christianity, together with the depiction of any of its symbols, which was strictly enforced by the Tokugawa military dictatorship for over three centuries after the year 1613, spelled the premature end of the introduction and adaptation of European techniques and themes in painting, copperplate engraving, and in music. All of these had reached an encouragingly high standard by the close of the sixteenth century. A Jesuit report of 16 September 1594, describing the work of the seminary of Arima in Kyushu stated: "There were this year in the seminary about one hundred pupils, divided into three classes of Latin, written and oral, of writing, Japanese and Latin, and of chanting and playing musical instruments. Those of the first class can already compose and recite therein, reading some lessons in a masterly manner, and they can perform some dialogue plays in Latin. Twenty students will graduate this year. . . . The painters and those who engrave on copper-plate become daily more skilful, and their works are but little inferior to those which are brought from Rome."[48]

Admittedly, Valignano, writing some seven years later, was considerably less enthusiastic about the Japanese potential for assimilating European culture in all its aspects. He stressed the difficulty which the students experienced in learning Latin and the strong distaste which they evinced for the study of this language. Whenever they were allowed to do so, they chose to study the Japanese classics rather than Latin, and they had almost to be forced to learn the latter. The complaints of Valignano were echoed by Padre João Rodrigues Tçuzzu and other Jesuit teachers; but the main difficulty may well have been the absurdly complicated Latin grammar of Fr. Manuel Alvares, which was the standard Jesuit textbook. In any event, real or alleged lack of fluency in Latin formed one of the chief stumbling blocks for the promotion of the *dojuku*, or catechists, to the priesthood, just as it did later in China. There were exceptions, of course, and the Japanese Jesuits of the early seventeenth century included several who were very fluent in Latin.[49]

Philippines

During the years when the Roman Catholic church was being savagely persecuted and virtually extinguished in Japan, save for the persistence of pockets of ''underground'' Christianity in a few remote rural areas, the Church Militant and Triumphant was consolidating and expanding its hold over the major portion of the Philippine Islands. The Spanish garrison in that remote region seldom numbered more than a few hundred effective men. The loyalty of some 600,000 Filipinos who had been converted to Christianity by the mid-seventeeth century was secured by some 250 regular clergy (Augustinians, Dominicans, Franciscans, and Jesuits) who were the parish priests and administrators of the mission towns and villages (*doctrinas*). Their role in this connection is examined further below; here we will consider briefly some of their reactions to the indigenous inhabitants and their cultural potential.

These reactions naturally varied in accordance with the character of the individual missionary, many of whom were favorably impressed by the Filipinos, although almost invariably in a paternalistic and rather condescending way. The much traveled Spanish Dominican, Fr. Domingo Fernández Navarrete, who spent nine years (1648–57) in the islands, after explaining that he and his colleagues took great trouble to learn the regional languages involved, added: "I always liked the Indians; they are not surly and stern, like those we saw in Mexico, but civil and tractable; they have wit enough and are very dexterous at anything. There are among them, excellent penmen, painters, carvers. They are apt to learn from and are very submissive to priests. As for their understanding in what concerns our Holy Faith, they may vie with many of our countrymen and outdo some of them. . . . They have excellent books in their language, which the Religious have printed, and they do love to read them; so this piety is owing to our labour and their aptness to learn. There is no Holy Day great or small, but abundance go to Confession and receive the Blessed Sacrament. I used to say, that the fervour of the ancient people of Castile was gone over to the Indian men and women at Manila. The Indians celebrate festival days very well, and all but a few of them dance very well; and so in processions they use dancing, and play well on the harp and guitar." As with Spanish missions in Mexico and Peru, tax exemption and other privileges were accorded to choristers and acolytes who helped with the celebration of the Mass; and the indigenous love of dance, drama, pagentry, and music was exploited to the full. [50]

Navarrete became very proficient in Tagalog—according to his own account—but he did not go so far in his appreciation of that language as did an earlier Jesuit missionary, Pedro Chirino, who wrote: "I found in this language four qualities of the four greatest languages of the world, Hebrew, Greek, Latin, and Spanish: it has the abstruseness and obscurity of the Hebrew; the articles and distictions in proper as well as in common nouns of the Greek; the fullness and elegance of the Latin; and the refinement, polish, and courtesy of the Spanish"—high praise indeed from a product of the High Baroque and the Catholic Reformation! Padre Chirino stressed how eager the catechumens, old and young, were to learn and chant the catechism (*doctrina*) by day and night. Those of them who were literate, "not only do they, as good students, write their lessons, mainly in their own characters, and using strips of reed as a book of memorandum and an iron point as a pen; but they always carry with them these materials, and whenever one ceases his labour, whether at home or in the field, by way of rest he takes his book, and spends some time in study."[51]

Despite their appreciation of the Filipino national character and cultural potential, neither Chirino nor Navarrete suggested that Filipinos were fit to be trained and ordained as regular clergy. Not only so, but the majority of missionary-friars and Jesuits in the Philippines strenuously opposed the periodic suggestions which were made for the formation of a well qualified indigenous secular clergy. Not a few Europeans and Creoles argued that the Filipinos were inherently unfitted for any sacredotal role, even as humble secular priests, being congenitally idle, vain, stupid, and, above all, unchaste. Others, while not going quite so far, argued that the Filipinos must always be treated as adolescents rather than as adults, even when they were fifty or sixty years old.

Widely differing viewpoints over the racial and cultural potential of the Filipinos were reflected in a celebrated controversy between the Augustinian friar Gaspar de San Agustin and the Jesuit Juan Delgado, both of them luminaries in their respective orders. Gaspar de San Agustin, O.E.S.A., who was quintessentially eurocentric despite (or because of?) his long residence in the Philippines, could not find a good word to say about the Filipinos, whom he considered were better fitted to be convicts and slaves than secular priests. His aguments, based essentially on the natural inferiority of all other races to the Western European, were devastatingly if urbanely demolished by Juan Delgado, S.J.; but most Spaniards in the Islands, whether laymen or religious, were inclined to agree with his Augustinian opponent. The result was that the sporadic efforts of the crown and of several archbishops to develop a well-educated indigenous secular clergy were hamstrung and handicapped at every turn by the open or the covert opposition of those ecclesiastical and crown authorities who should have done most to help. [52]

Vietnam

Returning to Vietnam, we have seen that the main reason for the surprising success of Christian evangelism there, was the rigorous training and the high standards of the catechists, who lived together in tightly disciplined communities. Vietnamese converts also took readily to the religious plays and spectacles which were organized by the missionaries, and to the canticles composed in their own language. This process was aided by the romanization of written Vietnamese, termed *quôc-ngu*, which the missionaries evolved and taught to their neophytes. A Portuguese Jesuit who reported on the Tongking mission in 1647, claimed that the converts had totally abandoned all their former beliefs and that there was no trace of syncretism in their worship. He added that they were extraordinarily respectful and submissive to their spiritual Fathers, and very proud of their new religion, which they professed openly and without shame. They were very loving and charitable toward each other, as if they were all brothers. "In short, this is a nation which seems singularly fitted for the Law of Christ, . . . and we have great hopes of reaping a magnificent harvest." And so it proved in the long run. Recent events have shown that the foundations of Christianity in Vietnam were well and truly laid over three hundred years ago. [53]

We have seen that the attitudes of the missionaries to the many and varied peoples with whom they successively came into contact, ranged from the uncompromising *tabula rasa* approach, which was the norm in the sixteenth-century Iberian America, to the much more sophisticated and accommodating methods evolved by some of the Jesuit missionaries in China and southern India. Inevitably, by virtue of their vocation and their calling, the missionaries were more inclined to give than to receive in the cultural interactions briefly considered above.

Most of the missionaries were clearly concerned not only with keeping themselves ''unspotted from the world'' but from being unduly influenced by the religious beliefs of those whom they were trying to convert.

Moreover, regard for the purity of their own faith naturally prevented them from imparting to their actual or potential converts inconvenient facts or dangerous ideas which might lead them to question the validity of the missionary's own teaching. Thus the geographical works published by the Jesuits in late Ming China, which were reprinted and circulated until well into the nineteenth century, avoided all mention of the Reformation and of the religious wars in contemporary Europe. These carefully ''slanted'' works gave the impression that Europe was a highly cultured and peaceful region, over which a benign Roman pontiff exercized unchallenged spiritual authority. The European missionaries, being subjected themselves to a rigid censorship of the printed word in Spain and Portugal, could hardly be expected to disseminate in the mission-field facts and ideas which were anathema at home. Nevertheless, despite this self-imposed handicap, the missionaries of the Church Militant often did play a useful role in making the different peoples of the world aware of each other's cultural values, as our sampling of the relevant literature shows.

CHAPTER THREE

Organizational Problems

Although the church is, or ought to be, primarily motivated by spiritual concerns, it is also, even for devout believers, a human as well as a divine institution. Inevitably, it has had to contend with various organizational problems, some of them closely connected with each other, whether in the mission-field or outside it. The interplay of temporal and spiritual concerns had many aspects which cannot be analysed in the space available. This chapter is therefore limited to a brief discussion of four vital themes: (a) relations between the regular and secular clergy; (b) the mission as a frontier institution; (c) the two Iberian royal patronages of the overseas church; (d) the Inquisition and the Iberian missions.

REGULAR AND SECULAR CLERGY

One of the features which marked the development of the Roman Catholic churches overseas, was the tension which often existed between the regular and the secular clergy. The hierarchical constitution of the church necessitates that its organized activity should normally be under the control and direction of the bishops, as consecrated successors of the apostles, with the supreme authority vested in the pope, as the direct successor of Saint Peter. Once diocesan and parochial administration had been established, the parishes should be administered by secular clergy under the direct control, jurisdiction, visitation, and correction of the bishops. However, for obvious reasons, pioneer missionary work, whether in "heathen" states and kingdoms, or in regions newly conquered by the Portuguese and Castilian crowns, could not be carried out by secular parish priests. Consequently, the superiors of the religious orders were given by the papacy in 1522 an all-embracing (*omnimoda*) authority to exercise the pioneering work of conversion and parochial administration. For this purpose, they were granted extensive privileges by the Holy See, including a wide range of exemptions from episcopal control and direction, save only those acts which required episcopal consecration. [1]

The exercise of these privileges soon came into conflict with the implementation of the decrees of the Council of Trent (1563–64); for one of the Council's main objectives was to strengthen the authority of the diocesan prelate over every phase of religious life and ecclesiastical discipline within his territory. The ensuing conflict between the extensive privileges of the religious orders and the jurisdictional claims of the bishops was never fully resolved throughout the colonial period. Neither the papacy nor the two Iberian crowns were consistent in their respective attitudes, tending to support now one side and then the other. Finally, the exaggerated regalism of the second half of the eighteenth century tipped the balance in favor of the secular clergy and the bishops, since they were under tighter control of the crown.

The most obvious solution was to develop a secular clergy in sufficient numbers and with sufficient qualifications to take over the parishes from the regular clergy as soon as they were firmly established—say after two or three generations. In practice, however, this often took much longer, especially in the remoter and more inhospitable regions. Few Iberian secular clergy cared to emigrate to distant and notoriously unhealthy regions such as "the rivers of Guinea," the island of São Tomé, and Angola in West Africa, or to the Paraguayan Chaco in South America. The Iberian population in many overseas settlements was for long too small to provide enough candidates for the priesthood. When a Creole clergy eventually did develop in the more settled regions, its members usually preferred to minister to their kith and kin in the cities and the towns, rather than to act as missionaries in the jungle, bush, or scrub.

For reasons that have already been indicated and for reasons to be discussed, the Iberian crowns did not actively encourage the formation of an indigenous clergy in many areas. When they did so in some others, the tendency was to relegate this clergy to an inferior category, thus reinforcing the built-in superiority complex of the regular clergy. This, in turn, strengthened the reluctance of the religious orders to hand over their parishes to their secular colleagues, whether these latter were Peninsulars, Creoles, or indigenous priests.[2] The superiority complex of the religious orders dates from the Middle Ages. These orders had their ups and downs, of course, and their standards were not invariably high or well maintained. But the papacy, prior to the reforms instigated by the Council of Trent, tended to acknowledge explicitly or implicitly, the moral superiority of the ascetic, monastic, regular life over the rank and file secular clergy, thereby converting the latter into a second-rate or inferior category.[3]

Last not least, the very human wish to hang on to power made the regulars loath to surrender their position and their privileges. A Jesuit Provincial in Paraguay wrote to his headquarters at Rome in 1644: "Every year magistrates are elected and given splendid titles, nominally to direct and to administer the Reductions; but they are unable to innovate, or to punish, or to order anything without explicit permission of the Fathers. One may even say that they feel glorified by having received this useless power and the authority of carrying *varas* [staves or wands of office]. In this way, God has made us Princes of this land."[4] Or, as Luís de Camões exclaimed in his *Os Lusíadas* (Canto 4), "*O gloria de mandar, ó vã cobiça!*"

The Jesuits can be acquitted of the sin of covetousness, of which they were often and wrongly accused; but their whole history shows that many of them were very fond of exercising power and very reluctant in relinquishing it. Racial prejudice was also responsible for the regular clergy looking down upon the secular in the non-European world, as explained in Chapter 1. Apart from the often uneasy relationship between the regular and the secular clergy, the religious orders were frequently at odds with each other. Rivalry between the Franciscans and the Jesuits, for example, reached dangerous dimensions in various times and places, notably in seventeenth-century Japan and Paraguay. Similarly, relations between the Dominicans and the Jesuits were often the reverse of cordial, whether in the Iberian Peninsula or overseas. With a view to minimizing this internecine rivalry, the papacy and the crown sometimes intervened to define respective spheres of missionary activity more narrowly. In 1594, for example, Philip II partitioned the Philippine Islands into missionary districts, giving each of the orders then working there (Augustinians, Franciscans, Jesuits, and Dominicans) its own separate field of apostolic activity.[5] This undoubtedly was a sensible move; but it did not prevent friars and Jesuits from exchanging tart remarks in their respective pulpits at Manila. Due allowance must be made for the tropical climate affecting short-tempered Europeans; but one Dominican preacher denounced the Jesuits as "the cats of the Church who lapped up all the cream." Another accused the sons of Loyola of having done more harm to the mystical body of Christ than had the Arch-Heresiarchs, Luther and Calvin.[6]

On the other side of the world, António Vieira, the Jesuit court preacher (at Lisbon) and fervent missionary (in Brazil) observed sarcastically in one of his letters that the Dominicans lived for the church but the Jesuits died for her.[7] His voluminous correspondence from the Maranhão is full of complaints about what he termed the Jesuits' "continual and cruel war with the friars, who in this land are more unconstrained, more arbitrary, and more blinded by self-interest than they are in many others."[8] Not seldom, this rivalry extended to the converts and neophytes of the various orders; again with awkward and embarassing results in the mission-fields of the Far East.[9]

It would be invidious to try to apportion praise and blame in all these long-standing and sometimes trivial disputes. But I have the impression after reading masses of documentation, published and unpublished, in the course of nearly fifty years, that on the whole the Jesuits did have higher standards and were often more self-sacrificing than their colleagues in the other orders — although certainly not always and everywhere. The secular authorities, who were inevitably drawn into these disputes, often admitted the moral and intellectual superiority of the Jesuits, even when they were highly critical of them in other respects. For instance, Dom Miguel de Noronha, fourth Count of Linhares and an exceptionally able viceroy of Portuguese Asia (1629–35), informed the crown that whereas the friars at Goa were often intemperate in their pulpit declamations, the Jesuits were much more moderate and better behaved. This testimony is the more convincing as Linhares was in some respects very critical of what he considered to be the undue power and influence exercised by the Jesuits at Goa.[10]

In the last decade of the seventeenth century, King Pedro II of Portugal informed the viceroy of India that in order to induce more missionaries to work overseas, those who could prove that they had worked for eight consecutive years in the mission-field, would then be allowed to return to Portugal if they so desired. The viceroy, in acknowledging the receipt of this order, stated that he had informed all the Superiors of the religious orders at Goa of its contents, with the exception of the Jesuit Provincial. He added: ''When these Religious come out to the missions, they regard the place where they exercise their vocation as their true country. I am convinced they would be scandalized if it was suggested that they had any inclination to return home to Europe.''[11]

Turning to Spanish America, where the Jesuits arrived later (1566) than they did in Asia (1542) or in Brazil (1549), they never achieved in the viceroyalties of Mexico and Peru the overwhelmingly preponderant role which they did in Portuguese Asia, Brazil, and the Maranhào. In Spanish America, they had to compete with the much more strongly entrenched friars of the

Mendicant Orders. Nevertheless, their relative superiority over most of the friars was often acknowledged by qualified observers, from viceroys and bishops downward. Near the bottom end of the colonial scale, we may instance the Peruvian Indian, Felipe Guaman Poma de Ayala (c. 1526–c. 1615). He was not a mestizo, as is often alleged, but a full-blooded Yarovilca Indian, although he had a half-brother, Martín de Ayala, who was a mestizo and became an ordained priest, something rather rare in sixteenth-century Peru. Felipe Guaman, in his rambling and at times incoherent *New Chronicle*, has an interesting analytical discussion of the virtues and vices of the regular and secular clergy in Peru, of which he had plenty of experience in his long life. He had very little time for the secular clergy; but he accords high praise to the Jesuits and (in a slightly less degree) to the Franciscans for their unselfish spiritual and charitable work. On the other hand, he is bitterly critical of the Dominicans, the Augustinians, and the Mercedarians, denouncing them for their brutal, greedy, and immoral exploitation of their indigenous parishioners. The Jesuits, he states, were not only charitable and unselfish, but were learned and fine preachers, "especially the Spaniards, their fame being celebrated throughout the world and in this kingdom of the Indians. For this reason, whenever one of these holy Fathers of the Company of Jesus appears in any Indian town or village, all the Indians of both sexes rejoice, as do their children and infants; for they regard the members of this Order as the representatives of the God of Heaven." [12]

The relative superiority of the Jesuits, in so far as it existed, is not difficult to explain. Their demands on their novices were more rigorous, their training period was longer, and they were more ready to dismiss those who could not make the grade. Their education system was justly admired by friend and foe, at any rate until the early eighteenth century. Consequently, they were able to attract the best and brightest pupils to their schools and colleges, particularly in the Portuguese empire, where their influence, power, and prestige were even stronger than in Spain and its dominions, until Pombal destroyed them. On the other hand, their closely knit esprit de corps, and the basic conviction of most of them that the Society of Jesus was inherently superior to the Mendicant Orders was not always tactfully concealed. It is, perhaps, neither unfair nor uncomplimentary to say that the Jesuits tended to regard themselves vis-à-vis the other orders as a drill sergeant in the United States Marines would regard the United States Army. To change the military comparison slightly, the Company of Jesus could be termed the Guards Brigade of the Church Militant. Unsurprisingly, this superiority complex, even when it was justified, as it often was, did nothing to endear the Jesuits as a body to the friars or to the secular clergy. It sometimes led to a complacent arrogance, which was deplored by the more thoughtful members and even, on occasion, by the general of the Society.[13] It also helps to explain why the dissolution of the Society in 1759–72 aroused so little protest and so little outspoken indignation in the Roman Catholic church as a whole.

THE MISSION AS A FRONTIER INSTITUTION

The intimate connection between the missions of the regular clergy and the border or frontier problems of the Spanish America was the subject of a seminal article by Herbert E. Bolton some sixty years ago. Readers of this article will recall that it concentrates heavily on the missions in Northern Mexico and in California.[14] These, together with the Jesuit Reductions of Paraguay, are the ones which have been most intensively studied and are consequently the best known. But the mission as a frontier institution was a feature of Iberian colonisation in many climes and in many cultures, some aspects of which are briefly considered below.

In so far as the Spanish empire was concerned, the golden age of the frontier missions can be said to have begun with the *Ordinances concerning Discoveries (Ordenanzas sobre Descu-*

brimientos) promulgated by Philip II in 1573.[15] *El Rey Prudente*, the Prudent King, realized that the crown of Castile's domains had become overextended, as the revolt of the Netherlands and the inconclusive struggle with the Turks made perfectly clear. The silver of America was required to finance Spanish campaigns in the Mediterranean, Italy, and Flanders. It should not be wasted on wild-goose chases after *El Dorado*, or on subjugating savage tribes in unproductive areas. Moreover, Bartolomé de las Casas had not been long in his grave, and his influence was still perceptible, as was that of his fellow Dominican, Fr. Fancisco de Victoria, revered today as the founder of international law.

The Ordinances of 1573 forbade armed *entradas* or expeditions, such as those headed by Cortéz, Pizarro, Valdivia, Alvarado, and other classic *conquistadores*. The reponsibility for the pacification of the border regions was placed primarily on the missionaries of the religious orders, accompanied, where necessary, by small military escorts or garrisons. Their role would be purely defensive and limited to the protection of the missionaries and of the "reduced" Amerindians. When a region was thoroughly pacified and the converted inhabitants resettled in villages and agricultural communities, then the missionaries would hand over their responsibilities to the secular clergy and advance another stage into the interior. The use of the word "conquest" was forbidden and was replaced by "discovery" or "pacification." A term of ten years was commonly envisaged for the transition from savage nomadism to a settled Christian society, but the process often lasted much longer. In any event, as noted above, the regular clergy were often reluctant to hand over their converts to their secular colleagues, even when they themselves continued to push forward the moving frontier.

The mutual support given by the cross and the crown in frontier pacification and extension in Spanish America and in the Philippines was facilitated by the structure of the Castilian Royal Patronage (*Patronato*, or *Patronazgo Real*). This institution made the missionaries into servants of both church and king, or, as they liked to phrase it, "in the service of both Majesties" (*serviçio de Entrambas las Majestades*), as explained below. But although the missonaries and the soldiers usually worked closely together, some of the former maintained, as Las Casas had done on occasion, that the latter were not really necessary. They argued that the confidence of unsubdued or hostile natives would be better gained by unarmed missionaries working alone or in pairs. This was, however, a minority view. It was strongly controverted by a majority of the missonaries, as some typical examples will show. Wrote Padre Francisco de Figueroa: "It is an error and very rash to allege, through lack of experience, that (barring a miracle of God) something notable can be achieved in preaching to and converting these people without an armed escort of Spaniards (*sin escolta y brazo de españoles*): for the innate brutality and utterly barbarous customs of these Indians, demand in justice that they should be first be ruled, disciplined and subjugated."[16]

The same conviction was voiced by Padre Manuel Uriate, S.J., writing of the Mainaus Mission in the mid-eighteenth century: "It is about a hundred years since the Company tried to reduce these Indians: however, neither the blood nor the sweat of so many Jesuit missionaries has sufficed to do so without the support of the secular arm. . . . These barbarous peoples do not listen to the voices of the Gospel preachers unless they have first heard the sound of gunpowder."[17]

Virtually identical sentiments had been voiced by the pioneer Jesuit missionaries in Angola and in Brazil. "For this kind of people," wrote Padre José de Anchieta from Brazil in 1563, "there is no better way of preaching than with the sword and the rod of iron" (*espada e vara de ferro*).[18] Ten years later, Padre Gaspar Simões wrote from Luanda: "almost everyone here is agreed that the conversion of these barbarians will never be effected by love, but only after they have been subjugated by force of arms and become vassals of our lord the king."[19] Nothing would be easier than to accumulate similar sentiments from the mission-fields of the Church Militant, but one more will suffice. Fr. Antonio Margill de Jesús, a Franciscan missionary-friar with experience in Central America and New Mexico at the end of the seventeenth century, observed emphatically: "In no single kingdom, province, or district of this vast American continent have the Indians been successfully reduced, without the gospel preaching and the blandishments of the missionaries being reinforced by the fear and the respect which the Indians have for the Spaniards."[20]

Constantino Bayle, the twentieth-century Spanish Jesuit historian, argued from these and other examples that "where there was an armed escort, there Christianity was firmly planted. Where the missionaries entered alone and unarmed, they became martyrs and did not make any converts as a general rule."[21] Perhaps the exceptions were more numerous than Bayle was willing to allow. Apart from the Guarani Reductions of Paraguay, admittedly something of a special case, there were instances in Spanish America, in Brazil, in Angola, and in the Philippines, where unarmed and unescorted missionaries *did* achieve a lasting success. Moreover, the presence of Spanish soldiers on occasion served as a deterrent rather than as an inducement to listen to the "blandishments" of the missonaries. German, Flemish, and Italian missionaries in Paraguay, for example, sometimes found that actually or potentially hostile Amerindians would listen more readily to them when they realized they were not Spaniards.[22] In short, the situation varied according to the time, the place, and the nature of the peoples involved. If the more usual procedure was for the pioneer missionaries to be accompanied by a small escort, there were times when unescorted missionaries achieved solid success. I may instance Padre António Vieira, S.J., on a visit to the Serra de Ipiapaba in 1660, Father Samuel Fritz, S.J., in the upper reaches of the Amazon,[23] Fr. Juan de Plasencia, O.F.M., in the Philippines,[24] and some of the Italian Capuchins in Angola.[25]

Whether working alone, or, more commonly, in conjunction with the secular arm, it cannot be denied that the missionaries, whether friars or Jesuits, in many frontier regions were the mainstay of colonial rule. They were far cheaper and more effective than large and costly garrisons would have been. A viceroy of Mexico once observed: "In each friar in the Philippines, the king has the equivalent of a captain-general and an entire army." Nor was this mere hyperbole. We have already indicated that the governor of the Philippines in 1787 averred that "the experience of more than two centuries has shown that in all the wars, rebellions and uprisings that have occured, the Religious parish priests were the ones who contributed most to the pacification of the malcontents."[26]

The situation in Portuguese India, where the areas controlled by the Lusitanian crown were miniscule in comparison with the vast regions claimed by the two Iberian crowns in America, was nevertheless similar in some respects. The Macaonese Franciscan chronicler, Fr. Paulo de Trindade, writing his *Conquista Spiritual do Oriente* (*Spiritual Conquest of the East*) at Goa in 1638, observed: "The two swords of the civil and the ecclesiastical power were always so close together in the conquest of the East, that we seldom find one being used without the other. For the weapons only conquered through the right that the preaching of the Gospel gave them, and the preaching was only of some use when it was accompanied and protected by the weapons."[27]

Just as the missionary-friars and the Jesuits in the Philippines were reluctant to hand over their parishes to the secular clergy, whether Creole or Filipino, so the Jesuit and the Franciscan parish priests in the frontier districts of Bardez and Salcete adjoining the island of Goa, were loath to hand over their parishes to the *Brahmene* secular clergy, even when the latter were, or claimed to be, fully qualified. The Portuguese colonial government, in the persons of the viceroys and the archbishops of Goa, tended to support the regular orders in their stand. They did not trust the loyalty of the *Canarins*, as the local inhabitants

were pejoratively termed, even after the latter had been devout
Roman Catholics for several generations. Here again, political
motivation was reinforced by racial prejudice until the egalitarian
decrees of the Marquis of Pombal brought about a change of
policy.[28]

The general standard of the European and Goan clergy in
Mozambique was never very high, and that of the Dominican
missionary-friars in the eighteenth century was generally admitted to be deplorably low. Both the regular and the secular
priests nevertheless exercized great influence among the Bantu,
by virtue of their sacerdotal status and the sacro-magical
elements of their religion. Alexander Hamilton, the sharp-
tongued Scots Calvinist "interloper," writing about the Bantu
of Zambesia and the Mozambique littoral at the end of the
seventeenth century from personal observation, commented:
"They have large strong bodies and limbs, and are very bold in
war. They'll have commerce with none but the Portuguese, who
keep a few priests along the sea-coasts, that overawe the silly
natives and get their teeth (i.e., elephant tusks) for trifles, and
send what they get to Mozambique."[29]

The tenuous Portuguese position in these regions was maintained only through the action of these missionary-priests and
the functioning of the secular society of the *prazo*-holders.
These latter became increasingly africanized in the course of
time. The garrisons of Mozambique island, Senna, Tete, and a
few other so-called "strongholds" (*praças*) never totaled more
than a few hundred men, most of them sickly and ill-disciplined
convict-soldiers or *degredados*. But for the combined action of
the priests and of the *prazo*-holders, the feeble Portuguese
presence in Zambesia would have ended centuries ago.[30]

To recapitulate: whether we look east or west, the missionary-
friars and the Jesuits formed the principal pillars of the two
Iberian empires for successive generations. Alexander von Humboldt, with his unsurpassed authority and powers of observation,
noted in Venezuela: "the missionary-friars and some soldiers
occupy here as in the rest of South America, forward posts on

the frontier with Brazil.''[31] Nor was the empire-building (and
-consolidating) role of the church limited to the frontier missions, which, important and interesting as they were, can be
regarded in some ways as peripheral phenomena. In the
absence of substantial military garrisons anywhere in the
Iberian colonial world before the second half of the eighteenth
century, it was primarily the priesthood of the Roman Catholic
church which kept the Peninsular, the Creole, the mestizo and
the indigenous population alike, loyal to the crowns of Castile
and of Portugal, respectively.

IN THE SERVICE OF BOTH MAJESTIES —
PADROADO AND *PATRONATO*

The close and inseparable connection between cross and
crown, throne and altar, faith and empire, was a major preoccu-
pation of Iberian monarchs, ministers, and missionaries alike.
At the apogee of the reign of Charles V, a Castilian poet extolled
the ideal of ''one flock, one shepherd upon earth, . . . one
monarch, one empire, and one sword.''[32] A century later, the
most influential Portuguese Jesuit of his day and generation
assured his monarch that Portugal had been created by God for
the express purpose of spreading the Roman Catholic faith
around the world. ''And the more Portugal acts in keeping with
this purpose, the more sure and certain is its preservation; and
the more it diverges therefrom, the more doubtful and dangerous
is its future.''[33]

For centuries this union of the cross and the crown was
exemplified by the peculiar institution — the term is fair enough,
despite its association with slavery in the ''Old South'' — of the
royal patronage of the church overseas exercised by the Iberian
crowns: *Padroado Real* in Portuguese, and *Patronato* (or *Patronazgo*) in Spanish. The Portuguese *Padroado Real* can be
loosely defined as a combination of the rights, privileges, and
duties, granted by the papacy to the crown of Portugal as patron
of the Roman Catholic missions and ecclesiastical establishments

in Africa, in Asia, and in Brazil. These rights and duties derived from a series of papal Bulls and Briefs, beginning with the Brief *Dum Diversas* of Nicholas V in 1452, and culminating in the Brief *Praecelsae Devotionis* of Leo X in 1514. The scope of the Portuguese *Padroado Real* in the non-European world was for long only limited by the parallel rights, privileges and duties, conferred on the *Patronato Real* of the Castilian crown by another series of papal Bulls and Briefs, of which the most important was the Bull *Universalis Ecclesiae* of Julius II in 1508.[34]

The latest commentator on these Briefs and Bulls maintains that the popes could only have granted them if they had been misled deliberately by the Portuguese as to the true situation in West Africa in the second half of the fifteenth century, when the local Negro inhabitants for the most part were neither Muslims nor enemies of Christendom.[35] This may have been so with the initial papal pronouncements of 1452–56; but by 1514, the papacy, if it cared at all, must have been more accurately informed. It likewise could have been better informed about Spanish atrocities in the Caribbean, where the peaceful Arawaks of Hispaniola and the Bahamas were well on their way to extinction.[36] It seems much more likely, to use current jargon, that the papacy could not have cared less. The worldly Borgias and other Renaissance popes were primarily preoccupied with family aggrandizement, with European politics, with the Turkish menace in the Mediterranean and the Balkans, and (after 1517), with the rising tide of Protestantism. They certainly did not concern themselves closely with the evangelization of new and distant lands beyond the rim of Christendom. Successive Vicars of Christ saw no harm in letting the Iberian monarchs bear the expense of maintaining the Church Militant overseas in return for the privilege of controlling it. Even when the papacy became better informed about the true situation, it did not abrogate or annul the privileges it had so readily granted in 1452–1514.

More specifically, the Iberian monarchs were authorized by the papacy: (a) to erect or to permit the erection of all the cathedrals, churches, monasteries, convents, and hermitages within the spheres of their respective patronages; (b) to present to the Holy See a short list of suitable candidates for all colonial archbishoprics, bishoprics, and abbeys; and for lesser ecclesiastical dignities and offices, to the bishops concerned; (c) to administer ecclesiastical jurisdictions and revenues, and to veto papal Bulls and Briefs which were not first cleared through the respective crown chancery. These privileges meant that in practice every missionary prelate and priest, from the highest to the lowest category, could only take up his appointment with the approval of the Crown concerned; and he depended on that crown for his financial support.

Moreover, the crown could and did transfer, promote or remove such clerics; it could and did decide the limits of their jurisdiction; it could and did arbitrate in any conflict of jurisdiction between the ecclesiastical and the civil power, and among ecclesiastics themselves. In many respects, therefore, the Iberian colonial clergy could be and often were regarded as salaried crown officials—just as happened with the Calvinist clergy employed by the Dutch East and West India Companies. The power and the influence of the pulpit, vitally important in the days before newspapers, radio, and television, were placed at the disposal of the crown, wherever and whenever the latter deemed this to be necessary. There were, of course, outspoken clerics who did not hesitate to criticize the crown's procedures or actions on occasion; but they could always be silenced or removed at short notice if the crown so wished. In other words, the colonial church was under the direct and immediate control of the crown concerned, save only in matters of dogma and doctrine.

The relative indifference of most sixteenth-century popes to the overseas missions, an indifference shared, incidentally, by the long drawn-out Council of Trent (1545–63),[37] was not shared by their seventeenth-century successors. Pope Urban VIII (1623–44), in particular, was an enthusiastic patron of missionary endeavor; and he was anything but complacent to the claims of the crowns of Spain and Portugal. By this time the Papacy had become ruefully aware that the extensive privileges so freely granted to the Portuguese and Spanish monarchs for the asking, were in many respects highly inconvenient and actually or potentially subversive of papal authority. As regards the Spanish colonial empire, successive popes could do very little to avoid working through the Castilian crown's *Patronato Real*. In fact, the papacy steadily lost ground in this respect, since several eminent Spanish canon and civil lawyers, beginning with the celebrated Juan de Solórzano Pereira (1575–1654), took a strongly regalist line under the Habsburgs. This tendency was intensified under their Bourbon successors, by such legal luminaries as Joaquin de Rivadavia, author of the *Manual Compendio de el Regio Patronato* (Madrid, 1755).

The Spanish Bourbons, under the influence of French Gallicanism and Regalism, claimed the right to exercise the *Patronato*, not merely by virtue of successive papal concessions, but as a direct consequence of their own sovereignty. Similar arguments were advanced in eighteenth-century Portugal, where the dictatorial Marquis of Pombal proclaimed (1774) that the king of Portugal, by virtue of his position as supreme head of the Order of Christ, was a ''spiritual prelate'' with jurisdiction and powers ''superior to all those of the diocesan prelates and the Ordinaries of the said churches in the East.'' Needless to say, the Papacy did not accept such absurdly extravagant claims; but its impotence was revealed for all the world to see by the suppression of the Society of Jesus in the Portuguese (1759–60) and Spanish (1767–69) empires, without their respective rulers obtaining the permission of the papacy. In Spanish America and the Philippines, the exercise of the *Real Patronato* continued in full force down to the wars of independence. This also occured with the *Padroado Real* in Brazil, where the Holy See was likewise unable if not unwilling to intervene.

It was a different story in Asia and in Africa. Spanish missionary-friars from the Philippines successfully challenged the monopolistic claims of the Portuguese *Padroado* in Japan and in China during the late sixteenth and early seventeenth centuries. They were followed by Italian and other missionaries sent out from Europe under the auspices of the Congregation of the Propaganda Fide, established at Rome in 1622 to coordinate and to supervise the missionary activity on a world-wide scale. There were also the French missionaries of the Missions Étrangères de Paris from 1658 onward. During the first half of the seventeenth century, the Dutch and the English East India Companies completely shattered Portuguese maritime power in Asian seas. There was no longer any obstacle to prevent the dispatch of missionaries who were not subject to the Portuguese *Padroado*, to anywhere in Asia, save to the modest territorial toe-holds retained by the Portuguese. Portugal's twenty-eight-year war of independence against Spain (1640–68), and her even longer and more debilitating colonial struggle with the Dutch (1596–1663), so weakened Portuguese resources in men, money, and shipping, that the *Padroado* missions were in a parlous plight. They could not possibly be adequately staffed and maintained from Portugal's exiguous resources alone, as Pope Innocent X pointed out forcefully to Padre Nuno da Cunha, S.J., the representative of the Portuguese Jesuits at Rome, in 1648.[38]

Weak as they were in reality, both in Europe and overseas, the self-styled "very high and very powerful" (*muito alto e muito poderoso*) Braganza monarchs fought a tenacious rear-guard action in defense of their original and cherished *Padroado* rights. They pointed out, correctly enough, that they had never prevented non-Portuguese missionaries from going to any of the *Padroado* missions, provided only that they sailed in Portuguese ships and acknowledged the jurisdiction of the Portuguese crown and of the *Padroado* prelates. But these two stipulations were precisely those to which many foreign missionaries increasingly objected. Richard Flecknoe, the English Roman Catholic poetaster and musician who was patronized by King John IV, declined the offer of a passage to India with the viceroy Count of Aveiras in 1650 on the ground that "not one Portugal

ship of three returns safe from that voyage, . . . the doubling
of the Cape of Bonna Esperanza being only dangerous at some
seasons in the year, which seasons they never avoid (by their
own confession) so unwise men, or so ill mariners are they, not
better to know to time their voyage or trim their ship.''[39]
Forty-four years later, an experienced Italian missionary-friar
was even more critical of the decline of Portuguese seamanship
and of the appaling mortality in the carracks and galleons of
carreira da India. He averred that any prelate who sent a
missionary out to India in a Protuguese ship should be regarded
as guilty of a mortal sin.[40] He may have been deliberately
exaggerating; but the mortality on Portuguese East Indiamen
was often very high for reasons which I need not discuss here.
Of 376 Jesuit missionaries sent from Portugal to China (via Goa)
between 1581 and 1712, no fewer than 127 died at sea.[41] As for
foreign (i.e., non-Portuguese) missionaries recognizing the
jurisdiction and the claims of the *Padroado*, many of them were
specifically prohibited by their respective governments from
doing so.

Although the papacy was increasingly determined to reduce
the scope and privileges of the *Padroado* after 1640, and
although it usually supported French, Italian, and Spanish
rivals where conflicts of jurisdiction occured, the exigencies of
European politics sometimes induced the Holy See to temporize
with Portuguese pretensions. In 1717, Pope Clement XI, who
had asked for and received Portuguese naval help for the
Venetians in their struggle with the Turks in the Aegean,
formally acknowledged that the three Chinese bishoprics of
Macao, Peking, and Nanking, were still within the sphere of the
Padroado. He also gave a half-promise (which he did not
implement) to create another three espiscopal sees in China on
the same terms. The official *Lisbon Gazette* jubilantly announced
that King John V — a great stickler for his *Padroado* rights — had
been reinstated as the ''despotic director of the missions of the
East,'' but this rejoicing proved premature.[42] The Holy See
continued to appoint vicars-apostolic to all the provinces of

China and in Indochina, without reference to Lisbon. Most of the Portuguese prelates in Asia, from the archbishop of Goa downward, gradually came into line with the Vatican's rulings. In West Africa, where the Italian Capuchins proved to be the most effective missionaries in the interior, the Portuguese crown agreed to cooperate with those sent out by the Propaganda Fide, as it did in the Cape Verde Islands and São Tomé.

Although rivalry between the Portuguese *Padroado* and the Castilian *Patronato* was often acute and at times inflamed by mutual xenophobia, there were also instances of close and cordial cooperation between missionaries of the two nationalities. The Jesuit mission in Japan, which was the most prized possession of the *Padroado*, was founded by a Basque and two Spaniards (Francisco Xavier, Cosmé de Torres, Juan Fernández). At the end of the sixteenth century, Spanish Jesuits still held the key posts in the direction of the mission, apart from the Portuguese Jesuit Bishop of Japan, Dom Luis de Cerqueira. [43] At the same period, the acting-governor of the Philippines, Luis Pérez Dasmarinas (1593–96), described the Portuguese bishop of Malacca, Dom João Ribeiro Gaio, as being most helpful and cooperative, ''and quite free of the quirks and pretensions of his nation.'' [44]

It should be noted in this connection that the Generals of the Society of Jesus at Rome, whatever their own individual national origins, always strove to make that Order a truly international one in the mission-fields of the Church Militant. To a large extent they succeeded; but they always had an uphill task, particularly where Portuguese, Spanish, and French subjects were involved. Portuguese and Spanish monarchs were always intensely jealous of the rights and privileges of their respective patronages; and Louis XIV yielded to nobody when it came to supporting French missionaries overseas, irrespective of their category or of their mission-field. The Jesuit Generals at Rome had a particularly difficult task in 1640–68, when Portuguese-Spanish rivalry was so embittered and so intense. The War of the Spanish Succession in 1702–1715 also caused them many headaches, since the Catholic Braganzas and Habsburgs were allied with the Protestant maritime powers against the Catholic French and Spànish Bourbons.

The Papacy likewise found it very difficult to maintain a balance between rival Portuguese, Spanish, and French pretensions in the mission-fields of Asia. This partly explains the zig-zag and wavering course that the Holy See sometimes followed in problems such as the Chinese rites. The cardinals of the College of the Propaganda Fide, who were subject to similar political and nationalist pressures, on the whole tended to support the Spaniards and the French, rather than the Portuguese. They took this attitude partly for reasons of state, and partly because they considered the quality of Portuguese missionaries to be lower, at any rate during the time of the influential secretary, Francesco Ingoli (1622–49), who was violently and outspokenly anti-Portuguese.[45] But, as noticed previously, whatever their misgivings about the functioning, or malfunctioning, of the Portuguese *padroado* and the Castilian *patronato*, the Vicars of Christ did not venture to abrogate or to annul the original Bulls and Briefs on which they were founded.

THE INQUISITION AND THE IBERIAN MISSIONS

Con el Rey y con la Inquisicion, chitón! ("Toward the King and the Inquisition, hush!") was a proverb with wide currency in both the Spanish and the Portuguese empires. The subject is one which obviously cannot be adequately covered here; but since the Inquisition was an arm of the Church Militant overseas in the two Iberian empires, a brief consideration of its activities is in order.

The Spanish Inquisition in the form which made it famous (or infamous) was established as a politico-religious institution during the reign of the "Catholic Kings," Ferdinand and Isabella. The objective was mainly to control potentially dangerous dissident elements, such as the recently (and forcibly) converted Moriscos and the *conversos* or "New Christians" of Jewish origin. Despite some initial opposition, particularly in Aragon, and despite papal reluctance, the Spanish branch of the Inquisition soon became not only in some respects a law unto itself, but a popular institution with the great bulk of the "Old Christian" community.

Inquisitorial functions in the New World were first handled by various prelates; but in 1570–71, two tribunals were established at Lima and at Mexico City, respectively, for the southern and the northern viceroyalties, the latter including the Philippine Islands. In 1610 a third tribunal was established at Cartagena de Indias. By an edict of Philip II in 1575, embodied in due course in the *Recopilacion* of 1683, the Amerindians were exempted from the jurisdiction of the Inquisition. They were not considered to be in the category of *gente de razón* ("intelligent people") in the same way as were Europeans, Creoles, and *mestizos*; and their conversion was considered to be too recent for them to attain the same knowledge and comprehension of the Faith. In practice, however, the Mexican and the Peruvian Inquisitions did sometimes take cognizance of Amerindian offences.

The Portuguese branch of the Inquisition was established in 1536, at the insistence of King John III, despite the prolonged hesitation of the papacy, which was only overcome by extensive bribery and backstairs intrigues. Since there was no Morisco problem in Portugal, the Inquisition at Lisbon, with branches at Evora and Coimbra, immediately concentrated on ferreting out real or alleged "New Christians," alias *conversos* or (more insultingly) *marranos*. Both the Spanish and the Portuguese Tribunals took cognizance of Protestant and other heresies, of witchcraft, sorcery, bigamy, sodomy, and sexual deviations. They likewise exercised, especially in Portugal, a rigorous censorship over the printed word. Protestants were never numerous enough to be a serious threat in the Iberian peninsula. Sexual offenses were not more harshly dealt with by the Inquisition than they were by the civil courts. Compared with the witch-hunters of seventeenth-century Old England and New England, the Iberian Inquisitors of the same period appear as positively enlightened in their attitude to witchcraft and sorcery. [46] It was on the detection and prosecution of crypto-Jews that the energies of the Iberian Inquisitors were concentrated, whether in the Old World or in the New. The Portuguese Inquisition never established a tribunal in Brazil or in Africa, contenting itself with the periòdic dispatch of visiting commissioners to those regions; but a tribunal was established at Goa in 1560, with jurisdiction over Portuguese Asia and East Africa. The Goa tribunal was under the remote control of the Chief Inquisitor at Lisbon, as the Spanish-American tribunals were under the jurisdiction of the *Suprema* at Madrid. Athough the Spanish Inquisition has achieved the greatest historical notoriety, the Portuguese Inquisition was regarded as being more rigorous and cruel by those unfortunate enough to have had experience of both institutions. [47]

The number of victims who died at the stake in the *Autos-da-Fé* (*Acts of Faith*) fades into insignificance when compared with the gas chambers of Hitler's "final solution," with Stalin's prison camps, and with other contemporary totalitarian horrors. The worst features of the Inquisitional judicial process were the refusal to give defendants the names of their accusers, or any indication of the extent of the evidence against them; and the efforts made, often with the use of torture, to induce them to incriminate others, beginning with their own families. As the English envoy at Lisbon reported in 1682: "Fathers and mothers, husbands and wives, brothers and sisters, are racked until by confession they become witnesses against the other, nor doth anyone know which of the others is in prison; and unless each confess every particular act of Judaism he or she has committed, the confession availeth nothing. As this proceeding looks very cruel on one side, so the Inquisitors say on theirs that nothing less can discover them, for that outwardly they profess the Romish religion, nor are they but very rarely circumcised." [48] The methods adopted by the Inquisition for collecting evidence placed a premium on the activities of informers, tale-bearers and slanderers. Private grudges could be paid off, merely by denouncing a man for changing his shirt, or a woman her shift, on a Friday night.

The procedure at an *auto-da-fé* was basically the same in the whole Iberian world, and the following eyewitness account of one held at Lisbon on 31 March 1669 may be taken as fairly typical.

There were three sorts of Judaisers: first, those against whom there was insufficient proof and who were dismissed on payment of charges. And these came out in black habits with a candle in their hands. The second sort, which came out in yellow coats with a red cross were accused and condemned in the manner following. ''The Deputies of the Holy Office of the Inquisition, etc., Whereas N. being a baptized Christian and obliged to live according to the Catholic faith hath lived according to the Law of Moses and expects salvation from thence, the evidence whereof appears in that he puts on a clean shirt on friday nights, fasts all saturdays till night, and will not eat either pig, hare, rabbit, or fish without scales *(these are the only proofs)*,[49] we declare him to be a Jew. But because he has acknowledged his crimes and promises for the future to obey the Pope and the Catholic Church, he is condemned only to lose all his goods.'' Immediately, he makes promise accordingly, and then by a stroke on the head with a rod, and the sprinkling of a little holy water they are made good Christians. Of the third sort, there was but one, a priest, who came out in a flaming coat, with his picture on the forepart of it (which afterwards is to hang up in the Dominicans Church). The proofs of his judaizing were the same as with the others, only it was added that he had confessed that he believed a man might be saved by either Law, and that therefore he sometimes observed the one, sometimes the other. Whereupon he was declared an apostate, and to be degraded, to lose all his estate, and to be punished according to the laws; in execution of which sentence, he was there degraded, and delivered to the secular justice who carried him to their own court, where by the judges he was asked whether he would die in the Law of Moses or of Christ, to which he answered in the Law of Christ, as he had always lived. He was therefore sentenced to be burnt to ashes, and the ashes thrown into the river, and that his name should be infamous; which sentence was presently put in execution; but because he said he would die a Christian he was strangled first.[50]

This eyewitness account brings out a point which has often been overlooked, at any rate until very recently. Many, perhaps most, of these "New Christians" wavered between the two faiths, practicing now one, then the other, or both simultaneously. This they did out of genuine uncertainty or indecision as to which was true faith, or whether (as in this particular case) the two faiths could in practice be reconciled with each other. Evidence of such vacillation is available in the records of the Portuguese Inquisition relating to Goa and to Brazil; and I presume it might be found in the Spanish-American documentation as well. [51]

The anti-Jewish phobia which was the hallmark of the persecutors, whether clerical or lay, is strikingly — and disgustingly — evidenced in the sermons preached at the *autos-da-fé*. Many of them were promptly printed in pamphlet form, and they evidently enjoyed a wide circulation. Readers wishing to sample the depths to which clerical bigotry, racial prejudice, and bestial brutality can descend, will find an excellent introduction to the subject in a definitive article by the late Professor E. Glaser. [52]

One interesting point which emerges from the nauseating monotony of this literature of hate, but which is not mentioned by Professor Glaser, is the role played by the women in the "New Christian" families in handing on the tradition of crypto-Judaism. The impression is given that it was mainly the mothers and the grandmothers who skillfully indoctrinated the children (who had, of course, been baptized and brought up as practicing Roman Catholics) when they reached the age of discretion. Statistical proof of this impression is inevitably lacking until thousands of the voluminous Inquisitional processes in the archives have been published in full. The position of women in Judaism was most definitely a subordinate one, as it was in all of Arnold Toynbee's so-called Higher Religions; but this subordination would not necessarily have prevented them from clinging to the vestiges of their ancestral faith with greater zeal than their menfolk. [53]

Vestiges, admittedly, was all that they could remember by the seventeenth century in regions where the crypto-Jews had no access to orthodox Jewish practices and synagogues. One

Christian preacher sneered at the Marranos for knowing only four or five out of a total of 613 precepts which they should have observed as orthodox Jews. The Portuguese bishop, Amador de Arrais, reproached the "New Christians" for being neither true Jews nor true Christians, since they observed neither faith in its entirety or purity. By attempting to practice both simultaneously, they merely rendered themselves doubly heretical.[54] Some orthodox rabbis would probably have agreed with him; since after the first generation of converts to Christianity had died out, their descendants had no access to Hebrew texts nor any possibility of preserving and observing the Law of Moses in its entirety. The progressive weakening of oral tradition with the passing of successive generations, and the Roman Catholic ambient in which they lived from birth to death, increasingly deprived the "New Christians" of all but the most basic vestiges of their ancestral faith. These included the name of *Adonai* for God, the belief that Jesus was an ordinary man and not the Messiah, and the dates of a few ritual feasts such as Purim and the Passover. Roman Catholic indoctrination of the children at school, and the unavoidably frequent attendance at church services, festivals and holidays, did not, as a rule, leave much room for more than a few simple and secret deviations from Christian practices. The only exceptions were those individuals who could travel abroad to places where Judaism was openly practiced, or more or less tolerated (Amsterdam, Rouen, Cochim, etc.), and there secure or renew the knowledge of their faith. Some men resorted to circumcision in such places; but this was a most dangerous step if they intended to return to any Iberian homeland or colonial settlement.

We have seen that the Inquisitors also took cognizance of sodomy and other sexual deviations, which they often investigated in the greatest detail, whether heterosexual or homosexual. Whether this was out of prurient curiosity or for some other motive I cannot say. In these days of "Gay Liberation," it is not always easy to recall the unmitigated horror with which Europeans of all creeds and classes regarded — or professed to regard —

the *peccado nefando*, as the Portuguese termed it. The "accursed sin" was usually considered by Catholics and Protestants alike as a crime which deserved the death penalty. This attitude was basically foreign to many Asian and Amerindian societies, with inevitable complications for the preaching of Christianity. It also led to some famous atrocities in the Iberian colonial world, such as the execution of Turan Shah, claimant of the throne of Ormuz at Goa in 1607, and Vasco Nuñez de Balboa's massacre of forty transvestites in the entourage of the Cacique Quarega in 1513. [55]

On the other hand, in dealing with sexual offenders at the very bottom of the social scale, the Inquisitors were sometimes more tolerant. From the confessions made at Pernambuco to the visiting Inquisitorial commissioner in 1594–95, it is clear that anal intercourse, whether homosexual or heterosexual, was the single most commonly confessed sin. But the Inquisitors do not seem to have been greatly concerned about the sexual mores of the lowest servile colored classes, regarding them as quasi- or non-persons, whose spiritual salvation was problematical and of little importance anyway. [56]

Another important function of the Holy Office was the censorship of books and manuscripts, in private as well as in institutional libraries. Lists of prohibited books were promulgated by the Spanish and the Portuguese branches of the Inquisition, as well as at the fountainhead in Rome. These lists varied in scope and contents, but they often included not only works by heretic or free-thinking authors, as also some by devoutly catholic writers. These latter included the playwright Gil Vicente, the chronicler João de Barros, and the devotional writer, Fr. Luís de Granada, O.P. It is sometimes argued that the Inquisition formed no real bar to intellectual achievement and original thought, since the Golden Age of Spanish literature and theatre roughly coincided with the years when the Spanish Inquisition was most active. This argument is of doubtful validity. The objective of the Spanish and Portuguese Inquisitions was not merely the preservation of theological purity and orthodoxy, but the suppression of any new ideas which might conceivably threaten or discredit Roman Catholic dogma as it was taught in the Iberian peninsula. [57]

Apart from anything else, the triple censorship exercized by the crown, the church and the Inquisition over all manuscripts submitted for publication after c. 1536, formed a barrier which must have discouraged many authors, particularly in Portugal, where the censorship was even more rigid than in Spain. As Fr. Francisco de Santo Agostinho de Macedo, O.F.M., a Portuguese Inquisitor with experience of the Holy Office in Italy and Spain, complacently observed in 1645: ''The vigilance [of the Inquisition] in ferreting out suspect doctrines is incredible; and it always was thus in this kingdom, where manuscripts have to be revised so often and approved by so many censors with such rigour, that this is one of the reasons why so few books are published here; and its lists of prohibited books are the most detailed and the most exact.''[58]

Lusitanian obscurantism was certainly a byword then and for long afterward. Whereas the Spanish monarchs allowed printing presses to function in their overseas possessions from relatively early dates (Mexico, 1539; Peru, 1584; Philippines, 1593), the Portuguese kings only sanctioned the functioning of a colonial press at Goa for about a century (c. 1556−c. 1676). Several attempts to start a press in Brazil (1706 and 1749) were swiftly scotched by the Portuguese government. Only after the arrival of the fugitive Braganzas in 1808, was printing allowed there. When Pombal was asked to consider the re-establishment of a press at Goa, he brusquely rejected the suggestion. Consequently, Portuguese missionaries in Brazil and in Africa had to send their catechisms, grammars, and dictionaries to Portugal for censorship, printing, and publication; a time-wasting and expensive procedure, which their Spanish colleagues could usually avoid. Those in Asia could sometimes get their works printed in places like Peking, which were outside Portuguese control and Inquisitorial vigilance, but these places lacked machine presses.

The golden age of the Iberian Inquisitors — if that is the right term — roughly coincided with the seventeenth century. This was the period of their greatest influence and activity, whether at Madrid or Mexico City, at Lisbon or at "Golden Goa." During the eighteenth century, the growth of regalism and of rationalism, the progress of the Enlightenment in its various forms, and the policy of anticlerical ministers at Madrid (Florida-blanca) and Lisbon (Pombal) combined to reduce the influence, power, and prestige of the Iberian branches of the Inquisition after about 1750. It is symptomatic of this decline that shortly before that date, a Portuguese Inquisitor was himself responsible for the clandestine reprinting of Luís Antonio Verney's *Verdadeiro Methodo de estudar* (1751). This work was highly critical of clerical obscurantism: and it had been banned, confiscated, and destroyed by the Portuguese Inquistion on its first publication five years earlier. Moreover, the offender received little more punishment than a mild reprimand. [59] Similarly, reiterated Inquisitorial bans on the importation of heretical and subversive books into Spanish and Portuguese America were increasingly evaded. They were almost totally ineffective during the last quarter of the eighteenth century. Many colonial private libraries, including those belonging to Roman Catholic priests, contained books by the Huguenot Pierre Bayle, by the radical polemicist Abbé Raynal, and by other precursors and exemplars of the French *philosophes*. Admittedly, these books did not circulate very widely, the great bulk of the people remaining illiterate, especially in Brazil; but successful revolutions are organized from above rather than from below. [60]

Summarizing the four organizational problems discussed in this chapter, we may, perhaps, hazard the following tentative conclusions. Although the tension between the regular and the secular clergy was not necessarily a bar to mutual cooperation, and might even foster a healthy rivalry between them, it was often productive of sterile ecclesiastical infighting. On the other hand, the Mission as a frontier institution was, on balance, remarkably successful, primarily in the wilds of Iberian America. The royal patronage exercised by the two Iberian crowns increasingly identified church with state in the seventeenth and eighteenth centuries, culminating in the exaggerated regalism of Bourbons and Braganzas. In the light of hindsight, this development can only be regarded as harmful to the spiritual health of the church overseas. Modern attitudes to the Inquisition will depend largely on the religious affiliations (if any) of the individual reader. But even those who—like myself—consider this to have been an odious institution, must acknowledge that its effective power had virtually disappeared by the end of the eighteenth century.

CHAPTER FOUR

A Tentative Balance Sheet

The reader who has persisted thus far in this survey of the expansion and consolidation of militant Iberian Christianity overseas, may feel inclined to ask what was the upshot of it all? Was it worth it? Did the missionaries achieve what they set out to do, and if not, why not? How far were they compelled to compromise with indigenous beliefs and observances?

Here again, the reader's own individual religious convictions (if any) are bound to influence his judgment. Moreover, some mission-fields have been much more intensively studied than others. If a great mass of documentation is now available in print, much more remains unpublished in the archives of Rome, Lisbon, Madrid, Seville, Goa, Mexico, etc. Many conclusions can only be tentative in the present state of our historical knowledge, and in view of the actual position of the Roman Catholic church in a rapidly changing world. But some very tentative conclusions may be formulated here, taking into special consideration three main (and continuing) problems: (a) the quantity and quality of the converts made by the Church Militant; (b) the persistence of idolatry and of synthetic Christianity; (c) the flow and ebb of missionary élan.

THE QUANTITY AND QUALITY OF THE CONVERTS

Shortly before leaving Malacca for Japan in June 1549, St. Francis Xavier wrote to the Jesuit missionaries in the Moluccas, giving them the guidelines they should observe when corresponding with their Superiors in Europe. They should write a detailed account of the work of conversion, "and let it be of edifying matters; and take care not to write about matters which are unedifying. . . . Remember that many people will read these letters, so let them be written in such a way that nobody may be disedified." [1] This injunction was usually strictly obeyed, especially when the letters and reports were intended for wide circulation, or for publication. Where they were not, the headquarters at Rome, Lisbon, or Madrid, normally edited the missives themselves before releasing them for wider circulation or publication. Due to this strict censorship, these carefully edited letters, valuable in many respects as they often are, must be used with a certain amount of circumspection.

Intended to whip up support for an interest in the mission, they often give the impression that things were going much better than they really were. Converts are numerous, intelligent, and spectacularly devout. Pagans are invariably worsted in arguments with Christians in general and with missionaries in particular. There is a general note of optimism, often verging on triumphalism. The impression is given that the conversion of uncounted thousands would be a relatively simple matter, if only there were more missionaries in the field to help reap the potentially rich harvest. The conversion of the ruler, whether the Great Mughal Akbar, the Manchu K'ang-hsi emperor, the "Emperor" of Monomotapa, or even the Dalai Lama of Tibet, is envisaged as a distinct possibility; thus affording glorious vistas of the mass conversion of all the ruler's subjects, in accordance with the encouraging precedent of the Emperor Constantine. By and large, the missionaries of the other religious orders took much the same line as did the Jesuits and for the same reasons — the edification of the faithful at home, and inducing more of them to volunteer for service in the missions overseas.

The combination of this evangelical euphoria with a fondness for round figures and a tendency to use the multiplication table frequently resulted in exaggerated estimates of the numbers of converts. Often no distinction was made between those people who were practicing Christians with a fair knowledge of their faith and those whose Christianity was merely nominal. Mass conversions were apt to be followed sooner or later by mass apostacies in regions where the secular power could not be used to support the spiritual, or where the indigenous ruler (or landowner) decided to persecute his Christian subjects (or tenants). Conversely, in regions effectively colonized or dominated, such as vast areas of Spanish America, ecclesiastical and civil authorities would work together to keep the converts in line.

While recalling once again Hilaire Belloc's aphorism that "all generalisations are false including this one," I may perhaps risk the following generalisations concerning converts in "Portuguese Asia," extending from the Cape of Good Hope to Japan. Muslims and Jews with a few insignificant and individual exceptions, remained impervious to Christian propaganda, save only where it was forcibly imposed, as on Muslim women taken in war. The same applied to Hindus, in so far as the higher castes were concerned. A notable exception was the mass conversion to Christianity in Goa and the surrounding districts of the bulk of the inhabitants, including the Brahmins by a mixture of carrot-and-stick methods between 1540 and 1570.[2] Similarly, the Buddhists of the Hinayana ("Little Vehicle") School remained basically unaffected by Christian evangelism in Burma, Siam, Laos, and Cambodia. Adherents of the Mahayana ("Greater Vehicle") School in Japan and China proved more responsive to the Gospel message, although I cannot explain why this should have been so. Culturally divided regions, such as Ceylon with its Hindu Tamils and its Buddhist Sinhalese, were likewise far from barren grounds, partly at any rate because the Portuguese destroyed the local temples and banished the indigenous priests.

I would hazard a guess that the total number of Christians never exceeded 300,000 either in sixteenth-century Japan or in seventeenth-century China, which formed, respectively, the golden years of those two missions.[3] The number of Christians in "Portuguese India" proper, can hardly have amounted to

200,000 at the most, with perhaps as many as 100,000 for Ceylon (Sri Lanka) when Portuguese power in that island was at its zenith. In the Philippines, some fifty years of intensive missionary efforts had resulted in about half a million Christians by 1622,[4] and the foundations of Philippine Christianity were firmly laid, outside of Muslim Mindanao, Jolo, and Sulu. For Vietnam, North and South, we may take a rough total of 300,000 by 1660, as previously noted.

There is no point in playing the numbers game in Spanish America, where conditions were very different from Africa and Asia. Effective Spanish control ensured that the christianization of the indigenous peoples in the conquered regions was swift and complete, at any rate outwardly.

More important than the quantity of the converts was their quality. This was a complex problem, both East and West. Obviously, many of the adults who were baptized *en masse* in places as far apart as Aztec Mexico and Hindu Goa were only superficially Christianized. The missionaries, or some of them, were under no illusions in this respect. But, as the pioneer prelate of Goa, the titular bishop of Dume, argued in 1522, even if the first generation of converts could hardly be expected to become good Christians, yet their children would become so with intensive indoctrination, and each successive generation would be more firmly rooted in the faith.[5] This, in fact, is just what happened in many regions, especially in those which were under effective Iberian control. Just as in Europe the descendants of the Saxons, Teutons, and Slavs who had originally been converted by forceful methods, in due course became fervent Christians, so the inhabitants of Central Mexico and of the Goa Islands, respectively, became profoundly attached to the religion which had been imposed, none too gently, on their forefathers. Inevitably, syncretic versions of Christianity tended to develop under these circumstances; but before briefly discussing this aspect, we may consider some of the more questionable methods which were employed by the Church Militant in order to obtain converts.

As mentioned above, in the reports which they circulated in Europe, the missionaries usually stressed the fervor, docility and adaptability of their converts; but in their confidential correspondence with each other and with their own Superiors, or with the secular power, they were usually much more frank. When, under the influence of Bartolomé de las Casas and his adherents, the Spanish crown had some passing thoughts of regarding the islands and mainland of the Ocean Sea as territory for a purely spiritual empire without the presence of numerous Spanish *conquistadores* and colonizers, a group of influential theologians at Lima reacted emphatically against implementing any such utopian idea. They argued that in the absence of a strong Spanish settler element, the Amerindians would promptly rebel and return to their former idolatrous practices, for the following reasons: (a) Because they had been born and bred in idolatry; (b) Because of the equivocal means used in their conversion; (c) Because of the "severity, serivitude, and unbridled greed" of which they were the victims; (d) Because of the "industry and persuasion of the Devil, who still deceives them with the vain hope that the Spaniards will leave this land, and they can then again be the lords and masters thereof, as they were before."[6]

This attitude was shared by the vast majority of those who thought about the problem at all; and it was often advanced as a justification for empire in the Iberian colonial world. Whatever abuse and mistreatment the converts suffered under the rule of the Castilian and the Portuguese crowns — and it was often admitted that abuses were both numerous and serious — nothing could justify a pull-out by the colonial power. This would inevitably lead to the relapse or to the destruction of the indigenous Christian communities formed under its sway and its protection. Padre António Vieira, S.J., in a celebrated sermon preached to his fellow missionaries in the Maranhão (1657) drew an allegory between the European Christian and the Amerindian, comparing the former to a statue of marble and the latter to a myrtle tree trimmed in human shape. The marble statue was more difficult to carve, by reason of the hardness of the stone; but once carved, it never altered. The myrtle tree was easy to cut or to trim, being of very malleable material; but unless the gardener clipped it constantly, within a few days it would produce sprouts which, if left unattended, would speedily grow and render the human form totally unrecognizable.[7] Neither church nor crown could contemplate abandoning a Christian community once it had taken root. King Philip II when advised to abandon the Philippine Islands as an unending economic burden for the Castilian crown, retorted that he would never do so while a single Christian hemitage remained there.[8] A similar line was taken by the Portuguese monarchs of the House of Braganza, when their Indian empire crumbled under the attacks of the heretic Dutch (1640–63) and the Hindu Marathas (1737–40), and some statesmen urged them to cut their losses.

The conviction that once people had been baptized and converted, they had become practising Roman Catholics in whom no backsliding or reneging on the faith could be tolerated, irrespective of the means used in their conversion, naturally led to serious abuses. Although the teaching of the church on the whole explicitly condemned the use of force to obtain converts, forceful methods were often employed and were justified by recourse to the biblical precept, *compele eos entrare*, ''compel them to come in'' (Luke 14: 16–24). I do not mean that converts were usually made at the point of the sword, or the sound of the gun, although this sometimes occured; and slaves were often baptized in the most summary fashion without any form of prior instruction.[9] But the more usual procedure was the suppression or the banishment of the indigenous priesthood; the destruction of ''heathen'' temples, whether Aztec, Maya, Hindu, or Buddhist; the burning and banning of all indigenous sacred texts; and the prohibition of any form of religious procession, rites, and services, save those of the Roman Catholic church, or what might be grudgingly tolerated (such as Hindu marriage ceremonies, on occasion) behind closed doors. This ''rigor of mercy'' as it was sometimes termed, amounted, in effect, to the use of force; especially when it was supplemented, as it often was, by compulsory attendance at catechumenical classes. Deprived of their priests, mullahs, shamans, or witchdoctors, as the case might be, and unable openly to practice the rites and ceremonies of their ancestral faiths, a cultural and religious vacuum was created in the subjugated indigenous communities. This vacuum could only be filled by conversion to Roman Catholicism, or by secretly practicing some form of more or less syncretic Christianity.

Although some missionaries disliked the use of forceful or of equivocal methods, there were other members of the Church Militant who had few scruples in this respect. If we can believe the sworn testimony of two Spanish Dominican missionary-friars, a particularly grave abuse was practiced in ''Golden Goa'' at the turn of the sixteenth-seventeenth centuries. Mass baptisms had long been practiced there; but these two eyewitnesses alleged that these ceremonies had become a tragi-comedy. They claimed that the Jesuits staged an annual mass-baptism on the Feast of the Conversion of St. Paul (25 January), for which occasion the neophytes were secured in the following way. A few days before the ceremony, the Jesuits would go through the streets of the Hindu quarter in pairs, accompanied by their Negro slaves, whom they would urge on to seize the Hindus, ''like greyhounds after a hare.'' When the blacks caught up with a fugitive, they would smear his lips with a piece of beef, thus causing him to lose caste and to become the equivalent of a pariah, or ''untouchable.'' Conversion to Christianity was now virtually his only option; but even then, the period of instruction was often limited to three days. The two friars further alleged that the Hindus had begun to counter this method by arranging for a special purification ceremony to be held in Hindu territory on the adjoining mainland, where those thus mistreated could purge themselves of their involuntary sin, ''even though, according to their own religion, this cannot be done.'' Dominican allegations against Jesuits should usually be taken with more than a pinch of salt; but we know from other contemporary sources that the Jesuits' practice of mass-baptism did arouse criticism and misgivings. [10]

The Christian Fifth-Column

Whatever the truth or otherwise of this particular allegation, the fact remains that many converts and their descendants became loyal subjects of church and crown. A chronicler of the Jesuit missions, Padre Fernão Guerreiro, observed in 1605: "As many heathen as are converted to Christ, just so many friends and vassals does His Majesty's service acquire, because these converts later fight for the State [of Portuguese India] and for the Christians against their unconverted countrymen." [11] This was largely, though not invariably, true; and it was something which caused concern to many indigenous princes and potentates at various times and places. The momentous decision of the Tokugawa government to implement the *sakoku* or "closed country" policy in 1639–40, was taken largely out of fear of an indigenous Christian "fifth-column," whose adherents might invoke Iberian military help, and supply cannon fodder for dissatisfied *daimyo*. This fear was grossly exaggerated, but it was none the less real.

Toyotomi Hideyoshi, the de facto ruler of Japan, in 1587–98, justified his seizure of the cargo from the wrecked Manila Galleon *San Felipe* and the execution of several missionaries and their converts in 1597 by claiming that the missionaries were the vanguard and organizers of a Christian fifth-column, subversive of the whole Japanese social structure and religious ethos. Rejecting the protests of the Governor at Manila over this widely publicized martyrdom, Hideyoshi asked rhetorically: "If, perchance, either religious or secular Japanese went to your kingdoms and preached the religion of Shinto therein, disquieting and disturbing the public peace thereby, would you, as lord of the soil, tolerate this? Certainly not; and therefore by this you can judge what I have done." [12]

Nearly a century and a half later, the Manchu Yung-cheng emperor made a similar retort to the Jesuits at the court of Peking. "What would you say if I sent a group of Bonzes and

Lamas into your country in order to preach their doctrines? You want all Chinese to become Christians. Your religion demands it, I know. But in that case, what will become of us? Shall we become the subjects of your king? The converts you make will recognize only you in time of trouble. They will listen to no other voice but yours. I know that at the present time there is nothing to fear; but when your ships come by thousands, then there will probably be great disorders."[13]

Fair enough, in both instances, one may think nowadays. But naturally these retorts did not carry conviction to the closed minds to which they were addressed. These members of the Church Militant were convinced that their own activities were inspired by God, and therefore above human interference; whereas those of the adherents of pagan faiths were inspired by the Devil. Consequently, the latter could be (and should be) lawfully and forcibly suppressed, wherever and whenever the secular arm could be used in support of the ecclesiastical power.

Persistence of Roman Catholic Christianity

One final point may be mentioned in connection with the problem of the quality of the converts. This is the extraordinary persistence of Roman Catholic Christianity once it had been firmly implanted, even if in a very simple, or else in adulterated or syncretic forms. Protestant English and Dutch eyewitnesses of the sadistic persecution of the Roman Catholic converts in early Tokugawa Japan, marveled at the steadfastness of the simple folk at the stake. These included "little children of five or six years old burned in their mothers' arms, crying out 'Jesus receive their souls.' " This steadfastness, commented a censorious Calvinist Hollander, might rather be termed stubborness "because (in so far as Holy Writ is concerned) they know but little, and can only repeat a Pater-Noster and an Ave-Maria, besides a few prayers to the Saints."[14] Less impressive, but more bizarre, a group of Negro slaves who had escaped from Macao and taken refuge among the Chinese in Fukien province, continued to have their children (by Chinese women, presumably) baptized and their marriages celebrated by Roman Catholic priests from Macao, who visited them periodically.[15]

If we move once again with Sir William Temple, "from China to Peru," we find the equally exotic denizens of the Zambo republic of the Esmeraldas who behaved in a similar way. Descended from a mixture of shipwrecked West African slaves with local Amerindian women in 1570, they maintained their complete regional autonomy, but allowed Roman Catholic priests to come and minister to them occasionally.[16] Similarly, the runaway African slaves in the *quilombos*, or war camps of the Brazilian backlands, often retained an adulterated form of Roman Catholicism rather than revert entirely to their ancestral African beliefs.[17]

Protestant missionaries found this persistence of Roman Catholicism very baffling and very frustrating; considering, as many of them did, that Mariolatry and the cult of saints and images were even worse than undiluted paganism.[18] During the two centuries that the Dutch East India Company endured, its Calvinist *predikanten* (ministers) could never contend on equal terms with the Roman Catholic priests. The Eurasian communities of Batavia, Malacca, Coromandel, Ceylon, and Malabar, from the mid-seventeenth century onward, whenever they had the chance — and often at considerable risk to themselves — would leave the *predikant* preaching to empty pews while they heard mass, or had their children baptized, or their marriages celebrated by some passing Roman Catholic priest in disguise. From the Protestant viewpoint, the circulation of the two rival faiths was a religious equivalent of Gresham's Law, with "Papist idolatry" continually gaining ground at the expense of the "True Christian Reformed Religion."

Moreover, even where indigenous Christians became impatient of Iberian suzerainty or the colonial yoke, they did not wish, as a rule, to abandon the faith which the Church Militant had implanted in their forefathers. Thus, Dom Garcia II, king of Congo in 1641–66, while cordially allying himself with the Calvinist Dutch invaders of Angola, 1641–48, flatly refused to have anything to do with Protestant propaganda and he prided himself on remaining a loyal son of Mother Church. [19] Dom Mattheus de Castro, the bitterly anti-Portuguese *Brahmene* bishop of Chrysopolis, while inciting both the heretic Dutch and the Muslim Sultan of Bijapur to throw the Portuguese out of Goa, stipulated in both instances that the Roman Catholic religion should continue to be publicly practiced there with its full ritual and ceremonial. [20] Nor did Tupac Amaru II, leader of the great Amerindian rebellion in Peru, 1780–82, advocate the disestablishment of the Spanish colonial church and a return to the sun worship of his Inca forebears.

THE PERSISTENCE OF IDOLATRY
AND SYNTHETIC CHRISTIANITY

The previously quoted aphorism, "one man's religion is another man's superstition," is certainly applicable here. Many people would maintain that Christianity itself is a synthetic religion—an offshoot of Judaism blended with Greek and Roman elements among others. So little is really known of Jesus of Nazareth that it can be argued that Christianity as it subsequently developed was primarily the work of St. Paul, of Philo of Alexandria, and of the church fathers. Or, as Norman Douglas (?) sarcastically defined it: "that quaint Alexandrine frutti-tutti which goes by the name of Christianity." [21] Such a conception was, obviously, totally foreign to the adherents of the Church Militant, whether Roman Catholic or Protestant. For them the Bible was the fountainhead and the touchstone of truth, every word of Holy Writ having been recorded under divine inspiration.

Nevertheless, even in Europe, allegedly equated with the faith by Hilaire Belloc ("The Faith is Europe and Europe is the Faith"), what may be termed "folk-Christianity," permeated by pre-Christian beliefs, persisted for centuries. This fusion of Christian and pagan beliefs was widespread in the Iberian Peninsula, more particularly, perhaps, in Portugal. All kinds of practices linked to the ancient gods survived obstinately in the habits and beliefs of the people, especially among the peasantry, although by no means confined to them. Belief in fertility rites, witches, vampires, the evil eye, spells, and omens, was so deeply ingrained in all sections of society that the Portuguese branch of the Inquisition usually contented itself with making routine denunciations of such practices, or the infliction of relatively mild punishments. [22] In Spain, the Inquisitors may have been rather more rigorous; but although they certainly believed to some extent in witchcraft themselves, they did not get unduly excited about it, as did people in Northern Europe and in North America during the seventeenth century. In Portugal, where pagan survivals were strongest, the spirits of the dead were often believed to hover around the scenes of their earthly life. They were apt to do mischief to their descendants, if not propitiated by prayers and offerings. Belief in both black and white magic was widespread and long lasting. A medical work published by a *Minhoto* surgeon with long experience in Brazil, which went through two editions between 1735 and 1755, while abounding in denunciations of quack doctors and of charlatans of both sexes, likewise contains a lengthy list of remedies and recipes which rely heavily on sympathetic magic, including prescriptions for the cure of sexual impotence caused by witchcraft. [23]

Peru

Since pagan beliefs persisted so long and so strongly in Christian Europe in general and in the Iberian Peninsula in particular, it is not surprising that the Church Militant found itself engaged in a ceaseless struggle against deeply rooted indigenous beliefs overseas. A few examples must suffice. Recently, attention has been directed, and rightly so, to the remarkable persistence of the indigenous religions in Peru, despite the efforts of the Church Militant to suppress them. During the seventeenth century, the colonial church mounted several formidable ''search and destroy'' campaigns to eradicate pre-Christian beliefs and practices. The results naturally varied, being rather ĕffective in some districts, less so in others, while some regions never experienced these probing *visitas*. [24] In any event, religious coexistence or syncretism, was very common. Many Amerindians who regularly attended church, devoutly heard mass, heartily sang in the choir, and who were baptized, married and buried in the fold of Mother Church, likewise practised their ancestral rites and ceremonies — or some form of them — often with Roman Catholic additions and overtones. Like the unconverted Chinese and Japanese who saw nothing incongruous in acknowledging the validity of both Confucianism and Buddhism (together with Taoism in China and Shintoism in Japan), many Amerindians believed simultaneously in the Christian God, in their own pre-Conquest deities, and in the Devil in both his biblical and indigenous forms. Whereas the European Christian believed, or was supposed to believe, that "straight is the way and narrow is the path which leadeth to salvation," many non-Christians would have agreed with the Indian raja who said: "Truth is a jewel which has many facets."

One of the pioneer Jesuits in Peru exclaimed despairingly that the Amerindians "were like the Moors of Granada, in that all, or most of them, have only the name of Christians and practice only the outward ceremonies." A century later, things had not changed very much, if we are to believe the evidence of Dr. Lara Galán in 1677: "The idolatry of the Indians is more solidly implanted today than it was at the beginning of the conversion of these kingdoms." This was, however, an evident exaggeration. His colleague, Juan de Esquivel, was nearer the mark when he wrote in the same year: "I am convinced that the whole of this archbishopric is corrupted by idolatry." [25] But if the Roman Catholic church in colonial Peru found the extirpation of the indigenous beliefs a labor of Sisyphus, it did succeed in changing and adapting them to the extent that Mother Church was accepted as a mediatrix between the individual and the supernatural world. In Mexico, where the Church Militant was rather more successful in imposing Christianity in depth as well as in extent, the cult of the Virgin of Guadalupe provided a most satisfactory fusion of pagan and Christian beliefs for millions. [26]

Congo

It was a similar story elsewhere of syncretism, coexistence, symbiosis, fusion, or whatever term the reader prefers for the product of the confrontation between militant Christianity and the indigenous cults. The old kingdom of Congo was superficially christianized during the long reign of King Dom Afonso I (1506–43), who was an active and sincere propagandist of Christianity, and of Western material civilization, as filtered through the crown of Portugal and its emissaries, ecclesiastical and lay, in central West Africa. The story of the abortive attempt to make the sixteenth-century Congo a forerunner (in retrospect) of Meiji Japan has often been told, and the interested reader is referred to two excellent works by Georges Balandier and W. G. L. Randles, respectively. [27] Here it will suffice to recall that the acceptance of some elements of Christianity, the most important of which was baptism, by the Congolese did not signify total commitment, but a desire to attain greater knowledge and ritual efficacy. With the possible exception of Dom Afonso I, neither the rulers nor the people were ever disposed to abandon polygamy; and the missionaries totally failed in their efforts to persuade them to do so. The king symbolized the mystical union and the interdependence of ruler and country in the Congo. With the acceptance of Christianity, he underwent a double form of consecration during the coronation ceremonies; with the Christian style of investiture representing a modernist façade and a supplementary sanctification of his magical power.

After the collapse of royal authority as a consequence of the defeat and death of Dom Antonio I at the hands of the Portuguese and their Jaga allies in the battle of Ambuila (29 October 1665), the existing syncretic form of Christianity was debased and fragmented still further. The ensuing "time of troubles" culminated in the early eighteenth century in the curious Antonian movement, which was a remodeled and a completely Africanized form of Christianity. The foundress and prophetess of this cult was a young woman of aristocratic rank named Kimpa Vita, alias Dona Beatriz. When sick and on the point of death, she had a vision in which she dreamt that she became the personification of St. Anthony. She taught that the Congo was the true Holy Land, and that Christ had been born of a Black Virgin in São Salvador (Mbanza Kongo). She adapted certain Roman Catholic hymns and prayers, including the *Ave Maria* and the *Salve Regina*, but she exhorted her disciples not to venerate the cross, "because it was the instrument of the death of Christ." She aroused national feeling, raised messianic hopes, and predicted a golden age for a restored Congo kingdom if her teachings were accepted. Her preaching met with a good deal of popular support, but the Italian Capuchin missionaries finally succeeded in persuading the ruling Congo king, Dom Pedro IV, to arrest and execute her. She was sentenced to be burnt to death together with her infant son and her male "Guardian-Angel" — or paramour, as the Capuchins claimed. The victims died at the stake on the 2 July 1706, and Dona Beatriz, like Joan of Arc, perished with the name of Jesus on her lips. [28]

Mozambique

Religious syncretism and coexistence were likewise conspicuous on the opposite side of Black Africa. The fusion of Christian and Bantu beliefs in the coronation and enthronement ceremonies of the Congo kings was paralleled after 1629 by similar rituals in the coronation of the "Emperor" of Monomotapa, as the superficially Christianized paramount chiefs of the Karanga tribal confederation were grandiloquently termed. In East Africa, as in West Africa, the missionaries could make no lasting dent in the practice of polygamy. The acceptance of Christianity in the sacral kingly culture of the empire of Monomotapa was even more superficial than it was in the kingdom of Congo. In the Zambesi river valley and in the coastal region from Sofala to the Querimba Islands, where militant Christianity had to contend with Islam as well as with the indigenous Bantu beliefs, the fusion of the three faiths aroused the angry denunciations of the more active and conscientious missionaries. One of them, Fr. João dos Santos, O.P., author of the classic *Ethiopia Oriental*, proudly relates how he forcibly prevented a Swahili headman in Querimba from circumcizing his own Muslim sons; although the friar admitted that he owed his life to the headman's sister, who had nursed him devotedly through a dangerous illness. The Dominican also put a stop to the existing practice of Muslim women inviting their Christian female friends on Sundays and Saints' Days, "when they all sang, danced and feasted together as friendly as if they were all Muslims." He added that he had succeeded in abolishing this "pernicious practice" despite much local resentment and opposition from both Muslims and Christians. [29]

Although this militant Dominican friar was convinced that he had put an end to this amicable mixture of Christian, Muslim and pagan practices, in point of fact the mixture continued much as before. An edict promulgated by the Inquisition of Goa in 1771, denounced numerous "rites, ceremonies, and superstitious abuses," which were widely prevalent among the Christians of Mozambique. They included the Islamic custom of publicly exhibiting to the assembled relatives, friends and neighbors, the piece of cloth or linen stained with the evidence of the first coitus between a newly married pair. Other abuses condemned by the Inquisition included the ritual celebration of a girl's first menstruation by invoking the "Most Holy Name of Jesus"; superstitious rites connected with the health of expectant mothers and the baptism of new-born babes; funeral customs which involved a female slave sleeping in the bed of a recently deceased master with a male slave of the same household; and the widespread use of the *muave*, the indigenous method of summary justice. This last practice necessitated accused persons taking an infusion of the bark of a certain tree. If they did so without ill effects, they were adjudged to be innocent, and thereby entitled to dispose of the life and property of the accusers. These and other similar rites were not limited to newly converted Bantu, but were practiced by whites, mulattoes, and Goans as well. [30]

India and China

Moving over to Portuguese India proper, we find that syncretism and coexistence between the rival faiths of Hinduism and Christianity continued to some extent even in the territory immediately adjoining ''Golden Goa,'' where the converts and their descendants were under the watchful eyes of the archbishop, the Inquisitors, and the members of the religious orders. Successive ecclesiastical councils held at Goa from 1567 onward, strictly prohibited the public celebration of any form of religion save the Roman Catholic. These councils likewise placed severe restrictions on social intercourse between Portuguese families and their non-Christian neighbors, but these regulations were not always strictly observed. As late as 1725–31, when the vast majority of the inhabitants of Goa, Bardez, and Salcete had been devout Christians for generations, some of them were accused of participating in Hindu marriage ceremonies, not merely behind closed doors but publicly in the open. An Inquisitor writing in 1731 claimed that Hindu priests and well-educated Brahmins (*Bottos*) and *Gurus* (teachers) secretly came across the border to Christian villages. Here they discussed ''the doctrines of their sect with the men and women, persuading them to give alms to the said *pagodes* (temples) and for their decoration, reminding them of the good fortune all their forefathers had enjoyed as a result of supporting them. They tell them that because they have failed in the said obligation, they have been overcome by the misfortunes which they are now experiencing. By convincing them with these arguments, they induce them to give the said alms, and to go [across the border] to the said *pagodes*, and there make offerings and perform sacrifices and other diabolical ceremonies, abandoning the Law of Jesus Christ.'' This Inquisitor complained that many frontier regions had been perverted and demoralized in this way. In all probability, he was considerably exaggerating the danger, but it undoubtedly existed. [31]

The problems created by the missionaries — mostly Jesuits, but not all of them — who tolerated the Malabar rites in India and the Confucian rites in China, are too well known to need more than a passing mention here. The advocates of both forms of toleration were often accused by their critics, both then and later, of assimilating Christianity to Hinduism, or to Confucianism, rather than the other way round. Papal attitudes to these hotly debated problems, in which the learned world of Europe joined, oscillated considerably. The Chinese rites were finally and unequivocally condemned by Pope Benedict XIV in 1742. Two years later the same pope condemned most of the Malabar rites.

Philippines

Syncretism in the Philippines aroused no discussion in Europe, but the missionaries in those islands were naturally closely concerned with it. The late Professor Phelan has shown that pre-Conquest Filipino rituals and beliefs eventually lost their pagan identity and blended into popular or folk Catholicism. With the passing of time, this process acquired increasing intensity; but to this day in the rural Philippines an atmosphere of the miraculous and the supernatural permeates popular Catholicism — as it does elsewhere in the Iberian world. Fr. Tomas Ortiz, O.E.S.A., a missionary with considerable experience both in the Philippines and in China (1690–1742) suggested that some of the Filipino rituals propitiating the souls of the dead were derived from the *Sangleyes*, or Chinese traders from Fukien who had settled in the islands. He instanced the custom of beating drums, gongs, and bells during an eclipse of the moon, in order to prevent it being swallowed by a tiger, dragon, or crocodile. Despite the similarity of such ceremonies, it is more probable that they were of indigenous origin. In any event, Friar Ortiz took a reasonably relaxed view of such superstitious practices. He enjoined his colleagues to be very careful in investigating and uprooting them, for they did no great harm to simple and uneducated believers. [32]

THE FLOW AND EBB OF MISSIONARY ELAN

Gaspar da Cruz, a Portuguese Dominican missionary-friar and author of the first European book on China, began the prologue to his work in 1569 with the following exhortation: ''In order that the peoples might be summoned to hear the Gospel, as they ought to be before the end of the world (according to St. Paul and according to Christ through St. Matthew), God ordained the discoveries made by the Spaniards in the New World, and that done by the Portuguese in the navigation of India. By these means, God through his servants has converted many peoples newly to the faith, and He continues converting and will convert them, until the coming (as St. Paul the Apostle says) of the overflowing of the peoples; Israel being saved by conversion, Jews and Gentiles forming one flock, and thus all will form one pale of one holy and catholic Church, under one Pastor as Christ says.''

In the concluding chapter of his treatise on China, Gaspar da Cruz mentions several dire signs and portents, floods, earthquakes and the like, which had devastated whole regions in 1556. This is clearly an echo of the world's worst (recorded) earthquakes, which killed some 800,000 people in the Ming empire. The friar also alludes to the spectacular comet of March 1556, which is said to have hastened the abdication of the Emperor Charles V. Fr. Gaspar then piously and prophetically concludes: ''It might well be that this sign was universal throughout all the world, and that it signifieth the birth of Anti-Christ. For the world showeth great signs of ending, and the Scriptures in great part show that they are drawing nigh to being fulfilled . . . . Whether it is one thing or another, or whatever it please God, may God in His infinite mercy open the eyes of these peoples blinded with the ignorance of the truth, so that they may come to the knowledge of Him. And let us all pray that He may open a way to His servants for them to preach to these peoples, and thus to draw them to the reward of His Holy Church. Amen." [33]

Spanish America

This euphoric exhortation with its apocalyptic and millennial overtones reflects a burning conviction which was held by many missionaries of the Church Militant, literally — once again — from China to Peru. Nowhere was this more clearly evinced than in sixteenth-century New Spain, where the notion of the universal monarchy of the Spanish Habsburgs was fused with the Spiritual Franciscan tradition of apocalyptic mysticism in the minds of many pioneer missionary-friars. When Fr. Francisco de los Angeles, Minister-General of the Franciscan Order, bade farewell to the twelve friars who were leaving to undertake the conversion of the recently conquered Aztecs in 1524, he referred to their mission as the beginning of the last preaching of the gospel on the eve of the end of the world. Several of these pioneer friars, and of their immediate successors, were strongly influenced by the mystical and millennial teachings of the Abbot Joachim of Fiore (died, 1202), or by those later ascribed to him. So for that matter was Christopher Columbus. [34]

This apocalyptic mysticism, with or without a Joachimite tinge, certainly sharpened the already fervent zeal of the spiritual conquerors of New Spain, by convincing them that time was short. The results of their tireless zeal and élan were most impressive, even if we discount evident exaggerations, such as the claim that Fr. Pedro de Gante baptized Amerindians in Mexico City at a daily rate of 14,000. By 1559, in the whole of New Spain, the Franciscans had a total of eighty houses and 380 religious; the Dominicans, forty houses and 210 religious; the Augustinians, forty houses and 212 religious. In other words, less than a thousand missionary-friars were ministering to several million Amerindians, and the spiritual conquest of Mexico was virtually complete. [35]

The 1560s and the 1570s saw the end of the golden age of missionary endeavor in New Spain. Partly because the basic work of conversion was achieved; partly because the crown, the bishops, and the secular clergy were encroaching on the privileged position of the Mendicant Orders; and partly because the apocalyptic and utopian zeal which had inspired the earlier generation was noticeably cooled. It was certainly not dead; but for practical purposes its swan song was echoed in the writings of the Franciscan friar, Geronimo de Mendieta, at the close of the sixteenth century, which the late Professor Phelan has so acutely analyzed. Thenceforward, it was the frontier missions on the northern marches of New Spain which attracted the most fervent and self-sacrificing missionaries.

The spiritual conquest of Peru took a different course and was less complete than that of Mexico. Nor is this surprising. The physical obstacles were greater than in Middle America, and most of the indigenous peoples opposed the new faith with a deeper and a more sullen resistance. Moreover, missionary activity got off to a slower and less dynamic start. Francisco Pizarro, though certainly a convinced Roman Catholic, was no fervent advocate and supporter of missionary work, unlike Hernan Cortés, "the Moses of the New World" as friar Mendieta termed him. Contrast the pious humility with which Cortes received on bended knee the pioneer "twelve apostles," for whom he had specifically asked, with Pizarro's brusque dismissal of a friar's advocacy of conversion: "I have not come here for any such reasons; I have come to take away from them their gold."[36] The apocalyptic and utopian fervor which animated so many of the early friars in New Spain was largely lacking in those of Peru. There were, of course, a few individual friars who were comparable to their colleagues in Mexico. But it was a general complaint during the first three decades of colonial Peru that the friars who were best fitted for acting as *doctrineros* were few and far between. The secular priests, who were present in larger numbers, were mainly interested in economic gain and creature comforts.

In 1563, it was officially estimated that there were then no more than 350 ordained priests, both regular and secular, in the vast viceroyalty of Peru, which included the "kingdoms" of Quito and Chile, as compared with some 820–900 in New Spain. There was a considerable increase later; the Carmelite friar, Vázquez de Espinosa, giving a total (c. 1620) of some 236 houses, 2982 ordained priests, and 302 curates of Amerindians for the five religious orders (Franciscans, Dominicans, Agustinians, Mercederians, and Jesuits) working in the southern viceroyalty. Secular priests were, of course, more numerous.[37] Still, whatever the totals at any given period, and despite the fact that crown officials were apt to complain that Peru was priest-ridden, in reality the church's manpower was always insufficient to accomplish the spiritual conquest of Peru to the same extent that it was achieved in New Spain. For that matter, Latin-American Catholicism in gerneral has always been faced with this problem: an average of anything between 5000 and 10,000 communicants with only one priest to serve them, from early colonial times to the present day.[38] Hence the inevitable tendency to syncretism, as noted above.

Portuguese Empire

If the sixteenth century was the time when apocalyptic fervor and the dream of a Habsburg world monarchy inspired many Spanish missionaries, the seventeenth century saw the flowering of a Portuguese messianic and millennial movement, which held that the king of Portugal would become the head of a universal monarchy. The "sixty years captivity" of Portugal to Castile between 1580 and 1640, when the two crowns were united in the persons of the Spanish Habsburgs, coincided with the spectacular growth of the cult of Sebastianism. This belief originated with the conviction in the minds of many people of all classes that King Sebastian, who had been defeated and killed on the Moroccan battlefield of Alcacer-el-Kebir (4 August 1578) was not really dead, but would return one day to resume the throne and to lead the nation to new and unprecedented heights of glory. An English Capuchin friar from Brussels, who spent some months at Lisbon in 1633, wrote that all Portugal seemed to have gone mad about Dom Sebastião: "The Turks do not more firmly believe in their Mahomet, nor the Jews in their Messiah, nor the Welsh in King Arthur, than the Portuguese in general do in their Dom Sebastião: clergy, theologians, preachers, gentlemen, and Religious of all the Orders."[39]

This belief was reinforced among all classes by the wide circulation in manuscript of some obscurely worded doggerel prophecies known as the *Trovas de Bandarra* (rhymes of Bandarra), which anteceded the Sabastianist movement but became its Bible after 1580. Vaguely and cryptically worded, they foretold the coming (or the return) of a Redeemer-King, who would establish a world empire of right and justice — the Fifth World Monarchy prophesied in the Book of Daniel. This would be accompanied by the recapture of Jerusalem from the Turks, the overthrow of the Ottoman Empire and the reappearance of the lost ten tribes of Israel. It would culminate in the conversion of all unbelievers and heretics to Roman Catholic Christianity under the spiritual suzerainity of the pope and the temporal overlordship of the king of Portugal. The most famous and influential exponent of the idea that Portugal was destined to the Fifth Monarchy in the near future was Padre António Vieira, S.J., (1608–97). This enthusiastic champion of the Church Militant, in his New Year's Day sermon before King John IV and his court in 1642, concluded with the hope that the fratricidal struggle with Catholic Castile would soon be over. The Portuguese would then be able to bathe their swords in the "blood of heretics in Europe, in the blood of Muslims in Africa, in the blood of pagans in Asia and in America; thus conquering and subjugating all the regions of the earth under one sole empire, so that they may all, under the aegis of one crown, be placed gloriously beneath the feet of the successor of Saint Peter."[40]

Vieira's belief in Portugal as the Fifth Universal Monarchy was greatly strengthened by his own missionary experiences in the wilds of South America. He remarked on the exiguous number of missionaries who, even in the most favorable circumstances, would be available for evangelizing the teeming millions of three continents. He likewise stressed the virtual impossibility of catechising hostile cannibals armed with poisoned arrows, who would let nobody approach them in the depths of the Brazilian forest. From these premises he argued that the conversion of the whole world to Christianity could not possibly be expected from the labours of a few thousand European missionaries, however devoted and self-sacrificing. This consummation, so devoutly to be wished, must await the direct intervention of God, working through His chosen kingdom of Portugal as prophesied in the Old Testament and in the *Trovas de Bandarra.*

Vieira was far from being alone in his belief that a concordance between the Book of Daniel and the Revelation of St. John the Divine afforded the chief clue to the shape of world history. Other believers included Sir Harry Vane, one-time Puritan governor of Massachusetts, who perished on the scaffold at Tower Hill in 1662, and Sir Isaac Newton, the last great scientific mind to take these visions seriously. Millennial and apocalyptic beliefs were widespread in the seventeenth century among Christians of all denominations, but here we are only concerned with Iberian exemplars. On the opposite side of the Portuguese world from Vieira, another Jesuit, Fernão de Queiroz (1617–88), penned voluminous works at Goa in which he argued that the coming of the Fifth Universal Monarchy under the crown of Portugal was close at hand. His own calculations likewise derived chiefly from the Book of Daniel and the Book of Revelations, but were reinforced by the prophecies of a humble Jesuit lay brother Pedro de Basto (1570–1645), who was Queiroz's equivalent of Vieira's Bandarra. These calculations proved to be miscalculations, since they predicted that the Portuguese-ruled Fifth Universal Empire would be ushered in with the final overthrow of the Ottoman Empire in 1702.[41] Nor would it be difficult to instance other Portuguese missionaries, whether in

Asia, Africa, or America, who were similarly inspired by these messianic, apocalyptic, and ultranationalist ideas.

The point I wish to make here is that it was their fervent belief in these ideas which kept them resolute and optimistic in the most discouraging circumstances, when the heretic Dutch were tearing the Lusitanian Empire apart, and when indigenous princes and potentates from the Bantu kingdom of Congo to Tokugawa Japan were throwing the Portuguese out of their realms. Buoyed up by these burning convictions, the Portuguese missionary stalwarts of the Church Militant argued that the particular crisis through which they happened to be passing was the darkest hour before the inevitable dawn. This triumphalism admittedly had at times rather unpleasant overtones; as in the incredibly arrogant and blindly bigoted attitudes of several of the Portuguese Augustinian missionaries in Safavid Persia to the Armenian christian communities at Julfa and elsewhere.[42] Although these millennial beliefs gradually weakened during the eighteenth century with the infiltration of some aspects of the Enlightenment into Portugal and its empire, they proved surprisingly long-lived. In 1725 we find the archbishop of Goa, a singularly pugnacious prelate who quarreled fiercely with viceroys and Jesuits, firmly convinced that the inauguration of Portugal's universal monarchy was only a few years away. ''And the reason is because God has deliberately chosen the Portuguese out of all other nations for the rule and reform of the whole world, with command, dominion, and empire, both pure and mixed, over all of its four parts, and with infallible promises for the subjugation of the whole globe, which will be united and reduced to one sole empire, of which Portugal will be the Head.''[43] The regions where these messianic and millennial beliefs have lingered longest, albeit in greatly modified but still recognizable forms, are in the *sertões* or backlands of Brazil, more particularly in the São Francisco river valley and in the arid wastelands of the Northeast.[44]

Missionary Vocations and Missionary Elan

Of course, Iberian missionary élan was not aroused and sustained only by virtue of these apocalyptic beliefs, widespread and important as they undoubtedly were at certain times and places. A missionary vocation could come to a man early or late in life; and if some individuals had set their hearts from boyhood on converting the heathen, others did so much later. Many men who in due course became missionaries, originally entered a Religious Order for very different reasons; the desire for the spiritual salvation of their own souls, for a contemplative religious life, or simply for peace and quiet, or in order to get away from women. [45] The reading of the missionaries' letters from the field in colleges, refectories, and libraries, must obviously have aroused a missionary vocation in many men, although we can never know how many. Similarly, others who originally may have had no thought of volunteering for foreign missions, were induced to do so by the efforts of missionaries who revisited their respective homelands in order to secure new recruits for the Church Militant overseas. But for one reason or another some 15,000 Jesuits asked to be sent to the mission-fields overseas as testified by their original requests which are still extant in the Jesuit archives at Rome (the *Litterae-Indipetae*), as Fr. John Correia Afonso, S.J., informs us. Inevitably not all of them persevered, and not all of them reached their original destination. The English Dominican friar, Thomas Gage, who was recruited in Spain for the Philippine mission — largely by the prospect of leading an easy life there, if his own account can be trusted on this point — opted to stay with the fleshpots of Mexico and Guatemala, nor was such truancy at all uncommon. [46] On the other hand, superiors sometimes had difficulties with those of their subordinates who desired to leave the safe but humdrum missions where they were in order to embrace the prospect of martyrdom in a more dangerous one.

Incidentally, former soldiers often made excellent Religious, as reflected in the Spanish proverb, *fraile que fue soldado sale más acertado*—perhaps on the analogy of poacher turned game-keeper.[47]

In conclusion, I would reiterate that despite the progress of deism, rationalism, and secularism during the first half of the eighteenth century, many missions were still in a relatively flourishing condition at the time of the suppression of the Society of Jesus in the Iberian world, 1759–72. This traumatic event proved fatal to some enterprises, such as the Chaco and Paraguay missions, and it did lasting damage to many others. But Jesuit vocations had continued to be relatively numerous right up to the time that the blows fell. In the years 1754–58, for example, at least seventy-seven Jesuit missionaries of various nationalities, of whom forty-eight were Portuguese, sailed from Lisbon in Portuguese Indiamen for the *Padroado* missions in Asia.[48] On the other side of the world, thirty-six Jesuit recruits for the Paraguay mission (out of forty who had embarked) arrived at Montevideo from Cadiz in the very year that the Society was suppressed throughout the Spanish dominions.[49] Even where, as in northern New Spain, the frontier missions of the Franciscans and others continued to flourish, the cutting edge of the Church Militant was thenceforth seriously blunted. Whatever the human failings of the sons of Loyola in other respects, the impartial historian is bound to admit with Protestant Peter Mundy: "And to speak truly, they neither spare cost nor labour, diligence nor danger to attain their purpose"—*Ad majorem Dei gloriam.*[50]

If we seek to draw some very tentative conclusions from this brief analytical survey of the expansion and consolidation of the Church Militant under the patronage of the Portuguese and the Castilian crowns, we find that the lasting results varied enormously. They range from enduring mass conversions in some regions, of which sixteenth-century New Spain is the prime example, to total failure in other countries, such as Cambodia, where the number of indigenous converts could be counted on two hands. Some reasons for this variation are obvious enough—lack of adequate missionary personnel—and others have been mentioned or analyzed above. As regards the quality of the converts, this, too, varied widely, from purely nominal "rice-Christians" to the model converts in Vietnam who had discarded all traces of their paganism.

Of syncretism there was plenty; but too much emphasis should not be placed on this. For example, there is still much that is either basically or superficially Amerindian in the popular Roman Catholicism of Mexico and Peru. But more important than the obstinate survival of pre-Conquest autotoch-tonous beliefs, is the general acceptance of Roman Catholicism as the dominant element in contemporary religious beliefs, ritual, and practice. This was the work of the missionaries of the Chuch Militant, literally—and for the last time—from China to Peru. In Old Goa, for instance, the Indian Christians may still retain the caste system in practice, if not in theory; but their devotion to the church is deeper than that of the majority of their European coreligionists.

The flow and ebb of Missionary élan has likewise varied throughout the centuries; but the zeal of the champions of the Church Militant still survived in many regions at the end of the Old Regime, despite the mortal blow dealt to several flourishing missions by the suppression of the Society of Jesus in 1759–72. For better or for worse, Latin America is likely to remain basically Roman Catholic for the foreseeable future, despite the inroads made by Positivism, Protestantism, Communism, and so forth. In Africa and in Asia, Roman Catholics were always, and seem likely to remain, minority groups in their respective homelands—the Philippines alone excepted. But as the Japanese proverb reminds us, "When you talk about the future, the crows laugh," and I have no pretensions to be a prophet. The mere survival of these Christian minorities through the vicissitudes of over three centuries is a tribute to the work of the dedicated missionaries of the Church Militant in times past.

Notes

CHAPTER ONE

1. Gomes Eanes de Zurara, *Crónica do Descrobimento e Conquista da Guine,* chap. 24, most conveniently consulted in the annotated French translation by Leon Bourdon et al., *Gomes Eanes de Zurara, Chronique de Guinée* (Ifan-Dakar, 1960), p. 109.

2. Bourdon et al., ed., *Chronique de Guinée,* chap. 60, pp. 179–80.

3. Basilio de Vasconcellos, ed. and trans., *Itinerário do Dr. Jerónimo Münzer* (Coimbra, 1931), pp. 51, 61–62. Unfortunately, we know nothing more about these enterprising printers.

4. Francisco de Santa Maria, *O Ceo aberto na terra. Historia das Sagradas Congregaçòes dos Conegos Seculars de São Jorge em Alga de Veneza, e de São Iorge Evangelista em Portugal* (Lisbon, 1697),bk. 1, chaps. 18–20, is responsible for a lot of misleading information about Congolese educated in Lisbon, which found general acceptance until recently debunked by Antonio Brásio, *História e Missiologia. Inéditos e Esparsos* (Luanda, 1973), pp. 257–328.

5. Psalm 72 in the Authorized (King James) Version. Cf. Maria Leonor Carvalhão Buescu, *João de Barros. Gramatica da Lingua Portuguesa . . . reprodução facsimilada, leitura, introdução e anotações* (Lisbon, 1971), pp. 4–5, 240.

6. Brásio, *História e Missiologia,* pp. 308–13.

7. Georges Balandier, *Daily Life in the Kingdom of the Kongo from the 16th to the 18th Century* (New York, 1969), pp. 52–58; W.G.L. Randles, *L'Ancien Royaume du Congo des origines à la fin du XIXe siècle* (Paris, 1968), p. 151.

8. For some names and dates see Brásio, *História e Missiologia,* pp. 892–93.

9. Malcolm Letts, ed. and trans., *The Travels of Leo of Rozmital through Germany, Flanders, England, France, Spain, Portugal, and Italy, 1465–1467,* Hakluyt Society, 2d Series, vol. 108 (Combridge, 1957), pp. 106–7.

10. S. F. de Mendo Trigoso, ed., *Viagem de Lisboa à ilha de São Tomé escrita por hum piloto Portugues* (Lisbon, n.d.), pp. 51–2, for a typical example.

11. António Brásio, *Monumenta Missionaria Africana. Africa Ocidental,* 12 vols. (Lisbon, 1952–197?),vol. 3 (1953), pp. 492-95, 552–53. This work is cited henceforth as Brásio, *Monumenta Africa Ocidental.*

12. Brásio, *História e Missiologia,* pp. 726–34, and the sources there quoted.

13. Brásio, *Monumenta Africa Ocidental,* vol. 7 (1956), pp. 225–75, 360, 522–27, 562–65. Cf. ibid., vol. 8 (1959), p. 176, for the advocacy by the governor of Angola, Fernao de Sousa, of a seminary at Luanda, where the sons of the tribal chiefs (*filhos de Sovas*) and others could be educated, in 1632.

14. As graphically described by the chronicler, António de Oliveira de Cadornega, *História Geral das Guerras Angolanas, 1681*, ed. Manuel Alves da Cunha, 3 vols. (Lisbon, 1940–42), vol. 3 pp. 312–13.

15. The seminary of São Salvador was primarily an elementary school (*escola de ler e escrever*) for the children of the Portuguese residents and of Congolese nobles; but Latin and other courses were given for those students whose parents requested this. For a typical criticism of the Congolese colored clergy, see the denunciation of a "sacerdote crioulo, muito valido del Rey. Assi chamão là os que tem mistura de dous sangues, e como raramente esta massa inclina para a melhor parte, segunedo o que de ordinario vemos, homem vicioso publicamente" (*apud* Brásio, *Monumenta Africa Ocidental*, vol. 5, p. 612). The best study of the tension between the colored secular and the white regular clergy in Congo and Angola is by Louis Jadin, "Le clergé séculier et les Capuchins de Congo et d'Angola, 16ᵉ–17ᵉ siècles," *Bulletin de l'Institut-Historique Belge de Rome* 36 (1964).

Of course, here again there were exceptions, including Francisco Fernandes de Sousa, a Congolese priest from Soyo, trained by Italian Capuchins and educated and ordained at Lisbon. He was an active and successful missionary in the *sertão* (bush); befriended the Flemish Franciscan missionaries in 1673–74; and was later nominated a = canon of Luanda Cathedral, a post which he filled to the general satisfaction for many years.

16. A similar situation prevailed in colonial Brazil, for the reasons explained in C. R. Boxer, *The Golden Age of Brazil, 1695–1750* (Berkeley and Los Angeles, 1964), pp. 131–35, 179–81.

17. Fr. Ardizone Spinola, C.R., *Cordel Triplicado de Amor* (Lisbon, 1680); C. R. Boxer, *Race Relations in the Portuguese Colonial Empire, 1415–1825* (Oxford, 1963), pp. 56–57, and the sources there quoted. An autograph letter of Fr. Miguel de Apresentação, O.P., addressed to King John IV of Portugal in 1650, was sold at Sotheby's (London) on 9 April 1974 (p. 107 and item 678 of the sale catalogue). The cataloguer has misread *Canarins* as *Canarias* and thus makes the ludicrous error of stating that the friar rejected the offer to return to Mozambique, since he wished to work in the Canary Islands (which were hostile Spanish territory then).

18. Lorenzo Tramallo to Cardinal Barberini, Lisbon, 9 July 1633, *apud* J. Cuvelier and L. Jadin, eds., *L'Ancien Congo d'après les archives romaines, 1518–1640* (Brussels, 1954), p. 556. For general discussion of Portuguese missionary endeavors in Mozambique and Monomotapa see Paul Schebesta, S.V.D., *Portugal's Konquistamission in Sudöst Afrika* (St. Agustin, Siegberg, n.d., but preface dated May 1966).

19. For the above and what follows, see Boxer, *Race Relations,* pp. 67–68, and the sources there quoted, the most important of which are Carlos Merces de Melo, S.J., *The Recruitment and Formation of the Native Clergy in India, 16th–19th Centuries. An Historico-Canonical Study* (Lisbon, 1955), and Dom Theodore Ghesquière, *Mathieu de Castro, premier vicaire apostolique aux Indes* (Louvain, 1937). To these should be added Jacob Kollaparambil, *The Archdeacon of All-India* (Kottayan 10, Kerala, India, 1972), and Joseph Thekedathu, S.D.B., *The Troubled Days of Francis Garcia, S.J., Bishop of*

Cranganore, 1641–1659 (Rome, 1972). Although the most famous, the seminary of the Holy Faith, later integrated with the Jesuit College of St. Paul at Goa, was not the only one of its kind. All the religious orders in Portuguese India (Franciscans, Jesuits, Dominicans, Augustinians) maintained similar institutions for training indigenous secular priests in their respective colleges, when these were of any size or importance, and sometimes when they were not. A list of the Jesuit college-seminaries in Asia will be found in Francisco Rodrigues, S.J., *A Companhia de Jesus em Portugal e nas Missões, 1540–1934* (Porto, 1935), pp. 56–63.

20. R. B. Cunninghame Graham, *A Vanished Arcadia: Being Some Account of the Jesuits in Paraguay* (New York, 1901), p. 121.

21. R. Boudens, *The Catholic Church in Ceylon under Dutch Rule* (Rome, 1957); M. da Costa Nunes, ed., *Documentação para a história da Congregação do Oratorio de Santa Cruz dos Milagres do Clero Natural de Goa* (Lisbon, 1966).

22. Boxer, *Race Relations*, pp. 68–69, and the sources there quoted, to which should be added the notice under his name in Diogo Barbosa Machado, *Biblioteca Lusitana* (vol. 3, pp. 41–42 of the four-volume reprint edition, Lisbon, 1930–35), implying that he *did* get the Inquisition post, although the viceroy, writing in 1736, states that he did not.

23. C. R. Boxer, *The Portuguese Seaborne Empire, 1415–1825* (London and New York, 1969), pp. 256–57; Claudio Lagrange Monteiro de Barbuda, ed. *Instrucções com que El-Rei D. José I mandou passar ao Estado da India, o Governador e Capitão general e o Arcebispo Primaz do Oriente no anno de 1774* (Pangim, 1844).

24. Often reproduced, and most conveniently available in the translation of H. de la Costa, S.J. in Gerald H. Anderson ed. *Studies in Philippine Church History*, (Ithaca, N.Y., 1969), p. 73.

25. Cf. José A. Llaguno, S.J., *La Personalidad Juridica del Indio y el III Concilio Provincial Mexicano* (Mexico, 1963); Guillermo Figuera, *La Formación del clero indigena en la Historia Eclesiastica de America, 1500–1810* (Caracas, Archivo General de la Nación, 1965), although this book has an inordinate number of misprints.

26. For the texts of the various Peruvian Ecclesiastical Provincial Councils, with accompanying notes and commentary, see Ruben Vargas Ugarte, S.J., ed., *Concilios Limenses, 1551–1772*, 3 vols. (Lima, 1951–54).

27. Figuera, *La Formación del clero indigena*, pp. 336–59.

28. Text most conveniently accessible in Francisco Mateos, S.J., ed., *Obras del Padre José de Acosta, S.J.* (Madrid, 1954), being vol. 73 in the Biblioteca de Autores Espanoles (Continuación) of the Real Academia Española), pp. 517–18, 601–2.

29. See John Leddy Phelan, *The Millennial Kingdom of the Franciscans in the New World* 2d. ed., revised (Berkeley and Los Angeles, 1970), p. 69, for a slightly differently worded translation and a longer extract.

30. Much relevant documentation is published by Richard Konetzke, ed., *Colección de documentos para la formación social Hispanoamérica, 1493–1810*. 3 vols. in 7 (Madrid, 1953–62).

31. Alonso de la Peña Montenegro, *Itinerario para parochos de Indios* (Madrid, 1668), pp. 368-71.

32. This Caracas affair is fully documented in Figuera, *La Formación del clero indigena*, pp. 359-65, 411-25.

33. Magnus Mörner, *Race Mixture in the History of Latin America* (Boston, 1967), p. 44 n. 33, and source (Konetzke) there quoted. Cf. also R. Konetzke, ed., *Colección de documentos para la formación social de Hispanoamérica*, vol. 2, pp. 551, 691-93, 759-60, 763-64, 774-75, for the Mexico City and Guatemala situations.

34. Ruben Vargas Ugarte, S.J., ed., *Concilios Limenses, 1551-1772*, vol. 2 (1952), pp. 3-153, and p. v of the editor's preface.

35. Horacio de la Costa, S.J., "The Development of the Native Clergy in the Philippines," in Anderson, ed., *Studies in Philippine Church History*, pp. 65-104, and especially pp. 72-73. This singularly objective and well-documented article is likely to remain the standard work on this topic. He shows how the average Filipino priest received just enough education to resent the suspicion and contempt with which he was treated by the great majority of the Spanish missionary-friars and colonial officials, but not enough to perceive the real causes for such treatment, or how to rise above it. Race prejudice was at the core of the Spanish attitude.

36. George Elison, *Deus Destroyed: An Early Jesuit in Japan and China* (Cambridge, Mass., 1973), p. 56.

37. For Cabral's clash with Valignano and his pejorative views on the Japanese, see Michael Cooper, S.J., *Rodrigues the Interpreter: An Early Jesuit in Japan and China* (New York and Tokyo, 1974), pp. 53-54, 174, 179; Elison, *Deus Destroyed*, pp. 15, 16, 20-21, 54-56.

38. Hubert Cieslek, S.J., "The Training of a Japanese Clergy in the Seventeenth Century," in *Studies in Japanese Culture*, J. Ruggendorf, S.J., ed. (Tokyo, 1963), pp. 41-78.

39. For the above and what follows see C. R. Boxer, "European Missionaries and Chinese Clergy, 1654-1810," in Michael Pearson, ed., *Festschrift in Honor of* Professor Holden Furber (in press at U. of Hawaii). and the sources there quoted, the chief of which are François Bontinck, *La Lutte autour de la liturgie chinoise aux XVIIᵉ et XVIIIᵉ siècles* (Louvain and Paris, 1962), and Joseph Kraal, S.J., *China Missions in Crisis. Bishop Laimbeckhoven and His Times, 1738-1787* (Rome, 1964).

40. For an analysis of Rougemont's memorandum drawn up at Canton in December 1667, see Bontinck, *La Lutte autour de la liturgie chinoise*, pp. 113-20.

41. Boxer, "European Missionaries and Chinese Clergy."

42. Adrien Launay, ed., *Journal d'André Ly* (Hong Kong, 1906), pp. 233-36.

43. Henri Chappoulie, *Aux origines d'une Eglise. Rome et les missions d'Indochine au XVIIe siecle*, 2 vols. (Paris, 1943-48); Henri Bernard-Maître, S.J., "Le P. de Rhodes et les Missions d'Indochine," in *I.'Histoire Universelle des Missions Catholiques*, ed. Simon Delacroix 4 vols. (Paris, 1956-59), vol. 2, *Les Missions Modernes* (1957), pp. 53-69; Adrien Launay, ed., *Lettres de Fr.*

Pallu, 2 vols., (Paris, 1904); idem, *Documents sur le clergé tonkinois par Mgr. Neez* (Paris, 1925); idem, *Histoire de la mission de Tonkin. Documents Historiques*, 1, *1658–1717* (Paris, 1927).

44. Achilles Meersman, O.F.M., ''Bishop Valerius Rist, O.F.M., and Serafino Maria de Borgia, O.F.M., Missionaries in Cambodia and Cochinchina, 1724–1740,'' *Archivum Franciscum Historicum Vol.* 57 (Florence) (1964);288–310.

45. J. Margraf, *Kirche und Sklaverei seit der Entdeckung Amerikas oder: Was hat die Katholische Kirche seit der Entdeckung Amerika's theils zur Milderung theils zur Aufhebung der Sklaverei gethan* (Tubingen, 1865), proves this conclusively, reproducing the relevant papal documents in whole or in part. Pope Leo XIII's self-congratulatory letter to the bishops of Brazil on the (very belated) abolition of slavery there in 1888 is riddled with historical inaccuracies and totally unjustified claims of earlier papal opposition to Negro slavery. These fatuous claims were debunked by William R. Brownlow, *Lectures on Slavery and Serfdom in Europe* (London and New York, 1892), and more recently by John Francis Maxwell, *Slavery and the Catholic Church* (Chichester, 1975), pp. 115–119. Maxwell does not mention either Margraf's book of 1865, or Brownlow's of 1892, nor a highly relevant article by Rayford W. Logan, ''The Attitude of the Church and Slavery Prior to 1500,'' *Journal of Negro History* 17 (1932); 466–80. But, although he adds nothing new to what those previous writers have exposed, he brings the sorry tale of the church's complicity down to the present day.

46. *Apud* Charles Gibson, ed., *The Spanish Tradition in America* (New York, 1968), p.105.

47. C. R. Boxer, *Portuguese Society in The Tropics: The Municipal Councils of Goa, Macao, Bahia and Luanda, 1510–1800* (Madison, Wis., 1965), pp. 131–33, and sources there quoted.

48. First published in French at London in 1798, and in Portuguese at Lisbon in 1808, it is most accessible in the edition prefaced by Sergio Buarque de Holanda, *Obras Económicas* (São Paulo, 1966).

49. First published in Francisco del Paso y Troncoso, ed., *Epistolario de Nueva España, 1505–1818*, 16 vols. (Mexico City, 1939–42), vol. 9 *1560–63* (1940), no. 490, pp. 53–55.

50. The *Arte de Guerra do Mar*, published at Coimbra in 1555, was first reprinted from the sole surviving copy (in the National Library, Lisbon) in an edition edited by Querino da Fonseca and Alfredo Botelho de Sousa at Lisbon in 1937. See pp. 23–25 of this edition.

51. See Don Betancourt of Indiana University, ''Spanish Colonial Critics of Black Slavery: Controversy and Conclusions'' (Forthcoming), for a documented discussion of this problem.

52. For Sandoval's Portuguese sources and correspondence see C. R. Boxer, *Salvador de Sá and the struggle for Brazil and Angola, 1602–1686* (London, 1952; reprinted Westport, Conn., 1975), pp. 237–41. There is a reprint edition of the 1627 *Naturaleza* (which uses the 1647 revised edition title of *De Instauranda Aethiopium Salute*, by A. Valtierra, S.J., published at Bogotá, 1956 (Biblioteca de la Presidencia de Columbia, vol. 22). For St. Pedro Claver, see

Stephen Clissold, *The Saints of South America* (London, 1972), pp. 173–201.

53. C. R. Boxer, *A Great Luso-Brazilian Figure: Padre António Vieira, S.J.* Hispanic and Luso-Brazilian Councils, Diamante Series No. 5 (London, 1957; reprinted 1963), pp. 22–23, for Vieira's attitude to Negro slavery.

54. Peter Laslett, *The World We Have Lost* (1971) pp. 185–89.

55. N. Cushner, S.J., "Slave Mortality and Reproduction on Jesuit Haciendas in Colonial Peru," *Hispanic American Historical Review* 55 (Durham, N.C.) (1975): 177–99.

CHAPTER TWO

1. Peter Gay, *The Enlightenment: The Rise of Modern Paganism*, 2 vols. (New York, 1967), vol. 1, p. 170.

2. A. da Silva Rego, "Portuguese Discoveries and Modern Missionary Apostolate," first published in the proceedings of a conference at Stockholm in 1960 and reprinted in his *Temas Sociomissionologicos e históricos* (Lisbon, 1962), pp. 45–49. The expression *muita e desvairada gente* is from the Portuguese chronicler Fernao Lopes (c. 1380–c. 1460).

3. *Doutrina Christãa . . . de novo traduzida na lingoa do Reyno do Congo* (Lisbon, 1624). The author, Matheus Cardoso, S.J. (1584–1625), based his Portuguese text on an earlier Portuguese catechism of 1561. Cf. also António Brásio, *História e Missiologia. Inéditos e Esparsos* (Luanda, 1973), pp. 437–93.

4. *Doctrina Christiana y catecismo para instruccion de los Indios y de las de mas personas que han de ser enseñadas en nuestra Sancta Fé* (Ciudad de los Reyes, 1584). A copy in the Lilly Library, Indiana University, has a signed ms. note at the foot of the title-page by José de Acosta, S.J., to whom the authorship is sometimes attributed (*Exotic Printing and the Expansion of Europe, 1492–1840. An Exhibit*, Lilly Library Indiana University, 1972, p. 17, no. 14. Hereafter cited as Lilly Library, *Exotic Printing*).

5. Reprinted by Museu Nacional de Arqueologia e Etnologia in a facsimile edition with an introduction by D. Fernando de Almeida, *Cartilha em Tamul e Portugues* (Lisbon, 1970).

6. Georg Schurhammer, S.J., "The First Printing in Indic Characters" and "Ein seltener Druck. Der Erste gedruckte Tamulische Katechismus," two articles on pp. 317–31 of vol. 2 of his *Gesammelte Studien. Orientalia* (Rome and Lisbon, 1963).

7. Piet van der Loon, *The Manila Incunabula and Early Hokkien Studies* (forty-three-page reprint edition by the Philippine Historical Committee, Manila, of the original article in *Asia Major*, New Series, vol. 12, pt. 1 [London] [1966]). A facsimile edition of the Tagalog-Spanish catechism with an introduction by Edwin Wolf II was published by the Library of Congress in 1947. The Chinese catechism was reproduced in a facsimile edition with an introduction by J. Gayo Aragón, O.P., and translation and notes by Antonio Dominguez, O.P., at Manila, 1951.

8. Johannes Laures, S.J., *Kirishitan Bunko. A manual of books and documents on the early Christian mission in Japan*, 3rd revised and enlarged edition (Tokyo, 1957), pp. 37–39, 41–43.

9. Bernard de Nantes, O.F.M., *Katecismo indico da lingua Kariris* (Lisbon, 1709).

10. Xavier S. Thani Nayagam and Edgar C. Knowlton, eds., *Antão de Proença's Tamil Portuguese Dictionary A.D. 1679* (facsimile edition by E. J. Brill of Leiden for the Department of Indian Studies, University of Malaya, [Kuala Lunpur, 1966]).

11. Doi, Tadao, *Kirishitan Gogaku no Kenkyū* [*A Study of Japanese Christian linguistics*] (Tokyo, 1971), is one of many works by the doyen of Japanese scholars in this field.

12. On the cultural contributions of the exiled Jesuits in general see Miguel Batllori, S.J., *La Cultura hispano-italiano de los Jesuitas expulsos, 1767–1814* (Madrid, 1966), and on Panduro in particular, Thomas Niehaus, "Two Studies on Lorenzo Hervás y Panduro, S.J.," *AHSI* 44 (1975): 105–30.

13. J. F. Schwaller, "A Catalogue of Pre-1840 Nahuatl Works Held by the Lilly Library," *Indiana University Bookman*, no. 11 (November 1973), pp. 69–88, especially p. 78.

14. Lilly Library, *Exotic Printing*, p. 31, no. 57.

15. For the publications of the Jesuit mission-press in Japan see Johannes Laures, S.J., *Kirishitan Bunko*. For works by missionaries in the Philippines, China, and in all other mission-fields, see R. Streit, O.M.I., and J. Dindinger, O.M.I., et al., eds., *Bibliotheca Missionum*, 30 vols. (Aachen, and Freiburg, 1916–), in each volume under the sectional heading of "Ungedruckte Dokumente und Linguistika" as well as under the author and year of publication.

16. C. R. Boxer, "A Tentative Check-list of Indo-Portuguese Imprints," in *Arquivos do Centro Cultural Portugues*, vol. 9 (Paris, 1975), p. 573, no. 8.

17. António Fernandes, S.J., *Magseph Assetat idest flagelum Mendaciorum contra libellum Aethiopicum* (Goa, 1642), in Boxer, "A Tentative Check-list," p. 587, no. 25.

18. Fernão Guerreiro, S.J., *Relação Anual das coisas que fizeram os Padres da Companhia de Jesus nas partes da India Oriental, e no Brasil, Angola, Cabo-Verde, Guiné, nos anos de 1602 e 1603* (Lisbon, 1605), p. 128.

19. António Gomes, S.J., to João Marachi, S.J., Varca, 2 January 1648, *apud Studia Revista Semestral*, vol. 3 (Lisbon, 1959), p. 225.

20. For a recent but possibly not final evaluation of Las Casas and his work by Lewis Hanke and other specialists see Juan Friede and Benjamin Keen, eds., *Bartolomé de Las Casas in History: Toward an Understanding of the Man and His Work* (DeKalb, Ill., 1974). Professor Hanke's own books and articles on Las Casas are too numerous to list here, but his *Aristotle and the American Indians: A Study in Race Prejudice in the Modern World* (London, 1959), may be taken as typical.

21. Munro S. Edmundson, ed., *Sixteenth-century Mexico: The Work of Sahagun* (Albuquerque, N.M., 1973) will serve as a good introduction for those who feel disinclined to tackle the twelve-volume edition of Sahagún's *General History of the Things of New Spain,* trans. A. J. O. Anderson and C. E. Dibble (Santa Fé, N.M., 1950–63).

22. A. R. Pagden, ed and trans., *The Maya: Diego de Landa's Account of the Affairs of Yucatán* (Chicago, 1975).

23. Most conveniently in the edition edited by Francisco Mateos, S.J., *Obras del Padre José de Acosta, S.J.* (Madrid, 1954) (see citation at chap. 1, n. 28). See also León Lopetegui, S.J., *El Padre José de Acosta, S.J., y las Misiones* (Madrid, 1942).

24. Benjamin Keen, trans., *Alonso de Zorita: The Lords of New Spain* (London, 1965).

25. Irving A. Leonard, ed., *Alboroto y Motín de los Indios de Mexico del 8 de Junio de 1692* (Mexico City, 1932), pp. 131–32. See also Leonard's *Don Carlos de Sigüenza y Góngora: A Mexican Savant of the Seventeenth Century* (Berkeley and Los Angeles, 1929), and his *Baroque Times in Old Mexico* (Ann Arbor, Mich., 1966), pp. 193–228.

26. Robert Ricard, *La conquête sprirituelle du Mexique. Essai sur l'apostolat et les méthodes missionaires des ordres mendiants en Nouvelle-Espagne* (Paris, 1933), is still the classic work on its subject, but it should be read in the light of James Lockhart's comments in *Latin-American Research Review* 7 (Austin, Texas) (Spring 1972); 6–45.

27. *Apud* Antonio Baião, *A Inquisição de Goa. Introdução à Correspondencia dos Inquisidores da India, 1569–1630,* Academia das Ciências (Lisbon, 1945), pp. 320–21.

28. Letter of Pero de Almeida, S.J., d. Goa, 26 December, 1558, in A. da Silva Rego, ed., *Documentação para a história das missões do Padroado Português do Oriente, India,* vol. 6, *1555–1558* (Lisbon, 1951), pp. 470–71.

29. J. L. Saldanha, ed., *The Christian Puranna* (Mangalore, 1907); A. K. Priolkar, *The Printing Press in India: Its Beginnings and Early Development* (Bombay, 1958), pp. 17–18.

30. Paulo da Trindade, O.F.M., *Conquista Espiritual do Oriente,* ed. Félix Lopes, O.F.M., 3 vols. (Lisbon, 1962–67), vol. 3, p. 148.

31. Vincent Cronin, *A Pearl to India: The Life of Roberto de Nobili* (London, 1959).

32. Josef Wicki, S.J., ed., *Diogo Gonçalves, S.J.: História do Malavar* (Münster and Westfalen, 1955).

33. Josef Wicki, S.J., ed., *Tratado do Padre Gonçalo Fernandes Trancoso sobre o Hinduismo, Maduré, 1616* (Lisbon, 1973).

34. Josef Wicki, S.J., ed., *O Homem das 32 Perfeicões e outras histórias. Escritos da Literatura Indiana traduzidos por Dom Francisco Garcia, S.J.* (Lisbon, 1958).

35. Fernão de Queiroz, S.J. *The Temporal and Spiritual Conquest of Ceylon,* ed. and trans., S. G. Pereira, S.J., 3 vols. (Colombo, 1930), vol. 1, pp. 79–80, 116–18.

36. Padre André Pereira, S.J., to Dr. António Ribeiro Sanches, d. Peking, 10 May 1737, *apud* C. R. Boxer, "A Note on the Interaction of Portuguese and Chinese Medicine in Macao and Peking, 16th-18th Centuries," in *Medicine and Society in China,* ed. John Z. Bowers and Elizabeth F. Purcell (New York, 1974), pp. 22–37.

37. C. R. Boxer, "Portuguese and Spanish Projects for the Conquest of Southeast Asia, 1580–1600," *Journal of Asian History* 3 (Wiesbaden/Bloomington, Ind.) (1969): 118–36.

38. G. J. Hudson, *Europe and China* (London, 1931), p. 242.

39. We have an excellent edition of Navarrete's work by J. S. Cummins, *The Travels and Controversies of Friar Domingo Navarrete, 1618–1686*, 2 vols., Hakluyt Society, (Cambridge, 1962). Gabriel de Magalhães, whose work was first published in French under a different title, *Nouvelle Relation de la Chine* (Paris, 1688, English translation *A New History of China,* London, 1688) has yet to find a modern editor, pending which we may hope for the publication of Irene Pih's Sorbonne thesis on this remarkable if rather abrasive character.

40. C. R. Boxer, ed. and trans., *South China in the 16th Century. Being the Narratives of Galeote Pereira, Fr. Gaspar da Cruz, Fr. Martin de Rada, 1550–1575*, Hakluyt Society (London, 1953), pp. xc-xci.

41. Renée Simon et al. eds., *Le P. Antoine Gaubil, S.J.: Correspondance de Pékin, 1722–1759* (Geneva, 1970), p. 695.

42. *Apud* C. R. Boxer, *The Christian Century in Japan, 1549–1650* (1951; reprinted Berkeley and Los Angeles, 1974), pp. 128–29.

43. Selections will be found *inter alia* in Boxer, *The Christian Century in Japan,* passim, and Michael Cooper, S.J., *They Came to Japan: An Anthology of European Reports on Japan, 1543–1640* (London, 1965), passim.

44. Michael Cooper, S.J., *This Island of Japan. João Rodrigues' Account of 16th-century Japan* (Tokyo and New York, 1973); idem, *Rodrigues the Interpreter: An Early Jesuit in Japan and China* (New York and Tokyo, 1974).

45. ". . . estes negros são diabólicos em seu governo" (Manuel da Camara de Noronha to the Viceroy Count of Linhares, d. Macao, 12 September 1633, *apud* C. R. Boxer, *The Great Ship from Amacon: Annals of Macao and the Old Japan Trade, 1555–1640* (Lisbon, 1959), pp. 129–30. Such pejorative use of the word "Negro" was far from uncommon. King John IV, writing to the viceroy at Goa in 12 March 1646, referred to the South Indian rajah of Quilon (Coulão) as a "Nigger," when this (admittedly rather minor) potentate insinuated that he would like to be officially recognized as a brother-in-arms of the King of Portugal (". . . como parece, advertindo ao Vicerey, entretenha este negro com boas palavras"). *Apud* Panduronaga S. S. Pissurlencar, ed., *Assentos do Conselho do Estado da India,* vol. 3, *1644–1658* (Bastorá-Goa, 1955), p. 479.

46. *Cartas que os Padres e irmãos da Companhia do Iesus que andão nos Reynos de Iapão escreverão,* 2 vols. in 1 (Evora, 1598), pt. 1, fl. 101. Letter of Aires Sanches, S.J., from Bungo, 11 October 1562.

47. *Ibid.* See also Mário Martins, S.J., *Os Autos do Natal nas Missões Portugueses do Japão,* twelve-page reprint from the review *Portugal em Africa,* no. 37 (Lisbon) (1950).

48. Francisco Pasio, S.J., letter of 16 September 1594, *apud* Boxer, *The Christian Century in Japan,* p. 205.

49. Boxer, *The Christian Century in Japan,* pp. 80–90, 194–95, 219–27.

50. *Apud* Cummins, ed., *The Travels and Controversies of Friar Domingo Navarrete,* p. 59.

51. Pedro Chirino, S.J., *Relación de las Islas Filipinas. The Philippines in 1600* (bilingual edition by Ramón Echevarria, Historical Conservation Society (Manila, 1969), pp. 41–42, 275, 149–50, 396.

52. For the Gaspar de San Agustin, O.S.E.A.–Juan Delgado, S.J., controversy over the national character and potential of the Filipinos, see Juan J.

Delgado, S.J., *Historia General Sacro-Profana, Política y Natural de las Islas del Poniente, llamadas Filipinas* (Manila, 1892), pp. 273–322. Cf. also Horacio de la Costa, S.J., "The Development of the Native Clergy in the Philippines," in *Studies in Philippine Church History* Gerald H. Anderson, ed. (Ithaca, N.Y., 1969), pp. 65–104; John Leddy Phelan, *The Hispanization of the Philippines: Spanish Aims and Filipino Responses, 1565–1700* (Madison, Wis., 1959), pp. 84–89.

53. For João Cabral's report, d. Macao, 12 October 1647, see Henri Bernard-Maître, S.J., in *L'Histoire Universelle des Missions Catholiques*, ed. Simon Delacroix, 4 vols. (Paris, 1956–59), vol. 2, *Les Missions Modernes* (1957), pp. 67–68. For the *quôc-ngu* see Maurice Durand, "Les Transcriptions de la langue vietnamienne et l'oeuvre des missionaires européens," in *Symposium on Historical, Archeological, and Linguistic Studies on Southern China, S.E. Asia, and Hong Kong Region*, ed. F. Drake and Wolfram Eberhardt (Hong Kong, 1967), pp. 288 ff.

CHAPTER THREE

1. The best short treatment of this subject, which I have followed very closely, is by Fr. Horacio de la Costa, S.J., "Episcopal Jurisdiction in the Philippines during the Spanish Regime," in *Studies in Philippine Church History*, Gerald H. Anderson, ed. (Ithaca, N.Y., 1969), pp. 44–64.

2. Robert Ricard, *La conquête spirituelle du Mexique. Essai sur l'apostolat et les méthodes missionaires des ordres mendiants en Nouvelle-Espagne de 1523–24 à 1572* (Paris, 1933), pp. 183–84.

3. C.N.L. Brooke, "The Missionary at Home: The Church in the Towns, 1000–1250," in *The Mission of the Church and the Propagation of the Faith,* ed. G. H. Cuming (Cambridge, 1970), pp. 59–83, and especially pp. 81–82, for the medieval European background.

4. *Apud* Magnus Mörner in *Hispanic American Historical Review* (May 1969), p. 337.

5. John Leddy Phelan, *The Hispanization of the Philippines: Spanish Aims and Filipino Responses, 1565–1700* (Madison, Wisc., 1959), pp. 49–50, for details.

6. E. H. Blair and J. A. Robertson, eds., *The Philippine Islands*, 55 vols. (Cleveland, 1903–9), vol. 25, 1635–1636, pp. 246–60.

7. The remark was made apropos of the Inquisition at Evora, but the Inquisition was primarily of Dominican origin, as Vieira implied elsewhere. Antonio Sergio and Hernáni Cidade, eds., *Padre António Vieira. Obras Escolhidas*, vol. 1, *Cartas* (1) (Lisbon, 1951), p. lvii; António Vieira, S.J., to King John IV, 8 December 1655, in J. Lucio d'Azevedo, ed., *Cartas do Padre António Vieira*, 3 vols. (Coimbra, 1925–28), vol. 1, p. 455.

8. Antonio Vieira, S.J., to the Father-General, G. Nickel, Rio das Almazonas [*sic*], 21 March 1661, in Serafim Leite, S.J., *Novas Cartas Jesuíticas* (São Paulo, 1940), p. 297.

9. C. R. Boxer, *The Christian Century in Japan, 1549–1650* (1951; reprinted Berkeley and Los Angeles, 1974), pp. 137–87; Henri Chappoulie, *Aux origines d'une Eglise. Rome et les missions d'Indochine au XVIIe siècle*, 2 vols. (Paris,

1943–48), passim; J. S. Cummins, ed., *The Travels and Controversies of Friar Domingo Navarrete, 1618–1686,* 2 vols., Hakluyt Society (Cambridge, 1962), index, s.v. "Jesuits."

10. *Diario do 3o* [*sic for 4o*] *Conde de Linhares, Vice-Rei da India,* 1 (all published) (Lisbon, 1937), pp. 36, 74, 135, 186, 203–5, 260.

11. Crown to Viceroy Count of Villa Verde, Lisbon, 23 January 1697, and Viceroy's reply of 23 January 1698 (author's collection). Cf. the analysis of the Bishop of Durango's report of 26 August 1715, on the excellent results achieved by the Jesuits in his diocese in northwestern New Spain as contrasted with the poor results achieved by the Franciscan missions, in Charles W. Polzer, *Rules and Precepts of the Jesuit Missions in Northwestern New Spain* Tucson, Ariz., pp. 54–57.

12. Luis Bustios Gálvez, et al, eds., *La Nueva Cronica y buen govierno escrita par Don Felipe Guaman Poma de Ayala,* 3 vols. (Lima, 1956–66), vol. 2, pp. 203–25, for the clergy of colonial Peru in his day.

13. Mutio Vitelleschi, S.J., *Carta a los Padres y hermanos de la Compañia de Jesus* (Rome, 2 January 1617).

14. *Hispanic American Historical Review* 22 (1917): 42–61. The latest of many works on this fascinating topic to come my way is the previously entered work by Polzer, *Rules and Precepts of the Jesuit Missions of Northwestern New Spain.*

15. Text in *Colección de documentos inéditos relativos al descubrimiento, conquista y colonización de las possessiones españolas en América y Oceania,* 42 vols. (Madrid, 1864–84), vol. 8 (1867), pp. 484–537, where date is erroneously given as 1563, and vol. 16 (1871), pp. 141–87.

16. *Apud* Constantino Bayle, S.J., in *Missionalia Hispanica,* vol. 8 (Madrid, 1951), pp. 418–19.

17. Ibid.

18. Anchieta to the Jesuit-General Diego Laines, d. São Vicente, 15 April 1563, *apud* C. R. Boxer, *Race Relations in the Portuguese Colonial Empire, 1415–1825* (Oxford, 1963), p. 22 n.

19. Gaspar Simões to the Jesuit Provincial, d. Luanda, 20 October 1575, in Boxer, *Race Relations,* p.

20. *Apud* Constantino Bayle, S.J., in *Missionalia Hispanica,* vol. 8, pp. 419–20.

21. *Missionalia Hispanica,* vol. 8, p. 421. Cf. Magnus Mörner's comments on Bayle's article in his *Political and Economic Activities of the Jesuits in Paraguay* (Stockholm, 1953), pp. 200–201, 214–215.

22. Philip Caraman, S.J., *Lost Paradise* (London, 1975), pp. 315–18.

23. George Edmundson, ed., *Journal of the Travels of Fr. Samuel Fritz, 1686–1723* (London, 1922).

24. Juan de Plasencia came to the Philippines in 1572 and died there in 1590. He was the author of the standard account of Tagalog customs and society.

25. Antonio Cavazzi de Montecuccolo, O.F.M. Cap., *Istorico Descrizione de . . . Angola* (Bologna, 1687).

26. E. H. Blair and J. R. Robertson, *The Philippine Islands,* 55 vols., (Cleveland, 1903–9), vol. 1, p. 42; Pedro Sarrió to the King, Manila, 22

December 1787, *apud* Horácio de la Costa, S.J., in Anderson, ed., *Studies in Philippine Church History,* pp. 72–73.

27. Paulo da Trindade, O.F.M., *Conquista Espiritual do Oriente,* ed. Félix Lopes, O.F.M., 3 vols. (Lisbon, 1962–67), vol. 3 chap. 26 p. 127.

28. Boxer, *Race Relations,* pp. 65–75, and sources there quoted.

29. Alexander Hamilton (1727), *apud* Boxer, *Race Relations,* p. 47.

30. Paul Schebesta, S.V.D., *Portugal's Konquistamission in S.O. Afrika* (Siegburg, 1966); Allen F. Isaacman, *Mozambique. The Africanization of a European Institution. The Zamberi Prozos, 1750–1902* (Madison, Wis., 1972); M.D.D. Newitt, *Portuguese Settlement on the Zambesi: Exploration, Land Tenure, and Colonial Rule in East Africa* (London, 1973).

31. *Apud* Constantino Bayle, S.J., in *Missionalia Hispanica,* vol. 8, p. 417. See also the extracts from Humbolt in Bailey W. Diffie, *Latin-American Civilization: Colonial Period* (New York, 1967), pp. 581–82.

32. Hernando de Acuña (1518–c. 1580), sonnet in praise of Charles. V and of his expansion of Christianity.

33. António Vieira, S.J., to King Affonso VI, d. Maranhão, 20 April 1657, *apud* C. R. Boxer, *The Portuguese Seaborne Empire, 1415–1825* (London and New York, 1969), p. 231.

34. Charles Martel de Witte, O.S.B., *Les Bulles Pontificales et l'expansion portugais au XVe siecle* (Louvain, 1958), is the standard monograph on this subject. For the text of *Universalis Ecclesiae,* see F. J. Hernáez, ed., *Colección de bulas, breves y otros documentos relativos a la iglesia de América y Filippinas,* 2 vols., (Brussels, 1879), vol. 1, p. 25, ff. For a general history of the Castilian patronate see W. E. Shiels, S.J., *King and Church: The Rise and Fall of the Patronato Real* (Chicago, 1961).

35. John Francis Maxwell, *Slavery and the Catholic Church* (Chichester, 1975), pp. 50–55.

36. Carl Ortwin Sauer, *The Early Spanish Main* (Berkeley and Los Angeles, 1966).

37. A. da Silva, S.J., trans. Joaquim da Silva Godinho, *Trent's Impact on the Portuguese Patronage Missions* (Lisbon, 1969), is inadequate, but the author admits that the Council gave no consideration to missionary problems, nor was the colonial church represented by any prelate attending the sessions. Much better is Josef Wicki, S.J., *Missionskirche im Orient* (Immensee, 1976), pp. 213–29.

38. *Apud* C. R. Boxer, *The Portuguese Seaborne Empire, 1415–1825* (London and New York, 1969), p. 233.

39. R. Flecknoe, *A Relation of Ten Years Travel* (London, 1656), p. 101. Flecknoe's decision was a wise one. Of the five sail with which the Viceroy Count of Aveiras left Lisbon in April 1650, none reached India that year, and the Viceroy died of fever near Quelimane in November. C. R. Boxer, "The Carreira da India, 1650–1750," *Mariner's Mirror* 46 (1960); 35–54.

40. Letter of Fr. Giovanni Battista Morelli Castelnovo, d. Surat, 15 December 1694, communicated to me by the late Dr. George Mensaert, O.F.M.

41. Joseph Dehergne, S.J., *Répertoire des Jesuites de Chine, 1552–1800* (Rome and Paris, 1973), p. 324 n. The great majority died at sea between Lisbon

and Goa. The voyage from Goa to Macao, with stopovers readily available at Cochim, Colombo, Malacca, and elsewhere, was not nearly so deadly as the *carreira da India.*

42. *Gazeta de Lisboa,* under dateline, Rome, 26 January 1718.

43. Of the thirteen padres assembled at Nagasaki for the Jesuit Congregation held there in 1592, only four were Portuguese. The five Spaniards attending occupied all the most responsible positions, and the remaining four were Italians. See A. Valignano, *Adiciones del Sumario de Japon,* ed. J. L. Alvarez-Taladriz (Tokyo, 1974), p. 678 n.

44. *Apud* C. R. Boxer, "Spaniards and Portuguese in the Iberian Colonial World: Aspects of an Ambivalent Relationship, 1580–1640," in *Liber Amicorum. Salvador de Madariaga,* H. Brugmans and R. Martinez Nadal, ed. (Bruges, 1966), pp. 239–51.

45. Henri Chappoulie, *Aux origines d'une Eglise. Rome et les misisons d'Indochine au XVII siècle,* 2 vols. (Paris, 1943–48), vol. 2, index, S.V. "Ingoli."

46. For the reluctance of the Portuguese Inquisition to interfere seriously with folk-religion and magic, see the suggestive essay by Donald Warren, Jr., "Portuguese Roots of Brazilian Spiritualism," *Luso-Brazilian Review* 5 (Winter 1968): 3–33.

47. Exemplified in I. S. Révah, "Le Plaidoyer en faveur des Nouveaux-Chrétiens portugais du licencié Martin Gonzáles de Cellorigo" *Revue des Etudes Juives,* 4th Series., tome 2 (122) (1963), pp. 279–398.

48. Charles Fanshaw to Sir Leoline Jenkins, d. Lisbon, 11 May 1682, in Public Record Office, London, SP89/14, fls. 199–200. This was written after Fanshaw had witnessed the *auto-do-fé* held on the 10 May 1682.

49. Parenthesis and underlining in the original.

50. Francis Parry to Joseph Williamson, d. Lisbon, 3 April 1669, in PRO, London, SP89/10, fl. 55.

51. Anita Novinsky, *Cristãos Novos na Bahia, 1624–1654* (São Paulo, 1972), pp. 141–62, "O homem dividido"; David Grant Smith, "Old Christian Merchants and the foundation of the Brazil Company, 1649," *Hispanic American Historical Review,* (May, 1974), pp. 223–59; C. R. Boxer, "António Bocarro and the *Livro do Estado da India Oriental,*" *Garcia de Orta* Numero especial (Lisbon) (1956), pp. 203–19; idem, "The commercial letter-book and testament of a Luso-Brazilian merchant, 1646–1656," *Boletin de Estudios Latino-Americanos y del Caribe Numero Especial . . . presentado a B.H. Slicher van Bath* (18 Junio, 1975), pp. 49–56; I. S. Révah, "Le Retour au Catholicisme d'António Bocarro," *Coloquio. Revista de Artes e Letras,* No. 10 (October 1960), pp. 58–60.

52. Edward Glaser, "Invitation to Intolerance. A Study of the Portuguese Sermons Preached at *Autos-da-fé,*" *Hebrew Union College Annual,* vol. 27 (1956) (New York, 1958), pp. 327–85; Rosemarie Erika Horsch, *Sermões Impressos dos Autos da Fé* (Rio de Janeiro, 1969), a useful bibliographical survey, but only the tip of an iceberg.

53. Arnold Wiznitzer, *Jews in Colonial Brazil* (New York, 1960); José Goncalves Salvador, *Cristaos-Novos, Jesuitas e Inquisição, 1530–1680* (São Paulo, 1969); Novinsky, *Cristaos Novos na Bahia.* C. R. Boxer, *Mary and*

Misogyny: Women in Iberian Expansion Overseas, 1415–1815 (London, 1975), pp. 56–58.

54. Amador Arrais, *Diálogos* (Coimbra, 1604). The author was Bishop of Portalegre, and the first edition was published in 1589.

55. The crown evidently did not feel too happy about the execution of Turan Shah, as a strongly worded royal decree of 1610 restored full rights and inherited privileges to his children (*APO*, 6, Nova Goa, 1875, doc. 105, pp. 841–42). For the transvestites who were torn to pieces by mastiffs on Balboa's orders, see Sauer, *The Early Spanish Main*, p. 232.

56. Patricia Aufderheide, "True Confessions: the Inquisition and Social Attitudes in Brazil at the Turn of the 17th [= 16th] century," *Luso-Brazilian Review* (Winter 1973), pp. 208–240, especially p. 219.

57. António Jose Saraiva, *História da Cultura em Portugal*, 3 vols., (Lisbon, 1950–62), vol. 3, pp. 108–89, for an excellent analytical discussion of the Inquisitorial censorship in Portugal.

58. Francisco de Santo Agostinho de Macedo, O.F.M., *Filippica Portuguesa contra la invectiva Castellana* (Lisbon, 1645), *apud* Saraiva, *Historia da Cultura em Portugal*, vol. 3, p. 188.

59. António Alberto de Andrade, *Vernei e a cultura do seu tempo* (Coimbra, 1905), pp. 462–63.

60. Mario Gongora, *Studies in the Colonial History of Spanish America* (Cambridge, 1975), pp. 159–205; E. Bradford Burns, "The Intellectuals as Agents of Change and the Independence of Brazil, 1724–1822," in *From Colony to Nation: Essays on the Independence of Brazil*, A.J.R. Russell-Wood, ed. (Baltimore, 1975), pp. 211–46.

CHAPTER FOUR

1. St. Francis Xavier to João de Beira, S.J., and the other Jesuits in the Moluccas, d. Malacca, 20 June 1549, in Georg Schurhammer, S.J., and Josef Wicki, S.J., eds., *Espistolae S. Francisci Xaverii aliaque eius scripta*, 2 vols., (Rome, 1944–45), vol. 2, pp. 108–15, especially p. 113. Cf. also Michael Cooper, S.J., *Rodrigues the Interpreter: An Early Jesuit in Japan and China* (New York and Tokyo, 1974), pp. 163–64; John Correia-Afonso, S.J., *Jesuit Letters and Indian History, 1542–1773* (Bombay, 1955, revised ed., 1969).

2. C. R. Boxer, "A Note on Portuguese Missionary Methods in the East, 16th-18th centuries, *Ceylon Historical Journal* 10 (Dehiwala, Colombo) (1965): 77–90, and the sources there quoted. Anthony D'Costa, S.J., *The Christianisation of the Goa Islands, 1510–1567* (Bombay, 1965), should be read in the light of the critical review in the *Bulletin of the School of Oriental and African Studies* 29 (1966): 399–401.

3. For Japan see C. R. Boxer, *The Christian Century in Japan, 1549–1650* (1951; reprinted Berkeley and Los Angeles, 1974), pp. 320–21, and for China, Francois Bontinck, *La Lutte autour de la liturgie chinoise aux XVIIe et XVIIIe siècles* (Louvain and Paris, 1962), p. 273.

4. John Leddy Phelan, *The Hispanization of the Philippines: Spanish Aims and Filipino Responses, 1700* (Madison, Wis., 1959), pp. 56–57.

5. Bishop of Dume to King John III, Cochin, 12 January 1522, in A. da Silva Rego, ed., *Documentação para a história das missões do Padroado Português do Oriente. India*, vol.1, *1499–1522* (Lisbon, 1947), pp. 452–53.

6. *Parecer* of 1567 *apud* Josep M. Barnadas, *Charcas. Origenes históricos de una sociedad colonial* (La Paz, 1972), pp. 176–77.

7. António Vieira, S.J., Sermon of the Holy Spirit, preached at São Luis do Maranhão, 1657. Unlike most of his contemporaries, Vieira did envisage in this sermon the possibility of the Brazilian Indians one day attaining the honours of the altar, and by implication, the priesthood. Cf. Maxime Haubert, *L'Eglise et la défense des "sauvages." Le Père Antoine Vieira au Brésil* (Brussels, 1964), pp. 153–55.

8. Magino Sola, S.J., in the preface, d. 12 February 1660, to Francisco Colin, S.J., *Labor Evangélica de los obreros de la Compañia de Jesus en las Islas Filipinas* (Madrid, 1663).

9. Cf. pp. 30–35 above.

10. Fr. Diego Aduarte, O.P., and Fr. Gabriel de San Antonio, O.P., memorial dated Valladolid, 8 February. 1605 (author's collection).

11. Fernão Guerreiro, S.J., *Relacam Anual . . . 1602 e 1603* (Lisbon, 1605), p. 110 (see full citation at Chapter 2; n. 18). The relevant chapter heading reads, significantly enough: "Of the service which the Company in all the aforementioned regions of the East renders not only to God by also to His Majesty and to the Crown of this kingdom."

12. On the *San Felipe* affair of 1596–97 and its aftermath, there is an enormous and continuing literature, of which it will suffice to cite Boxer, *The Christian Century in Japan*, pp. 163–67, 416–24; idem, *Indiana University Bookman*, No. 10 (November 1969), pp. 25–46; George Elison, *Deus Destroyed: The Image of Christianity in Early Modern Japan* (Cambridge, Mass., 1973), pp. 136–41, 159, 426–28; Michael Cooper, S.J., *Rodrigues the Interpreter*, pp. 132–59.

13. *Apud* C. R. Boxer, *The Portuguese Seaborne Empire, 1415–1825* (London and New York), p. 242.

14. Eyewitness accounts of Richard Cocks (1619) and Reyer Gysbertsz (1626) most conveniently available in Michael Cooper, S.J., *They Came to Japan: An Anthology of European Reports on Japan, 1543–1640* (London, 1965), pp. 388–89.

15. Bishop Palafox, *Conquest of the Empire of China by the Tartars* (London, 1671), pp. 8, 300–307; François de Rougement, *Relaçam do Estado político e espiritual do imperio da China, 1659–1666* (Lisbon, 1672), pp. 7–8.

16. John Leddy Phelan, *The Kingdom of Quito in the Seventeenth century* (Madison, Wis., 1967), pp. 3–22.

17. Jose Alipio Goulart, *Da Fuga ao suicidio. Aspectos da rebeldia do escravo no Brasil* (Rio de Janeiro, 1972); Stuart B. Schwarz, "The Mocambo: Slave Resistance in Colonial Bahia," *Journal of Social History*, no. 4 (Summer 1970): 313–33; Edison Carneiro, *O Quilombo dos Palmares*, 3rd ed. (São Paulo, 1966).

18. Among others who took this line, I may cite Jean Brun, *La Veritable Religion des Hollandois, avec une apologie pour la Religion des Estats*

Generaux des Provinces Unies (Amsterdam, 1675), and G. de Raad, *Bedenckin-gen over den Guineeschen Slaefhandel der Gereformeerde met de Papisten* (Vlissingen, 1665). I owe a Photocopy of this last exceedingly rare book, of which only two copies appear to be extant, to the kindness of Mr. Franz Binder.

19. Jan Vansina, *Kingdoms of the Savanna* (Madison, Wis., 1966), pp. 142–52; W. G. L. Randles, *L'Ancien Royaume du Congo des Origines à la fin du XIXe siécle* (Paris, 1968), p. 110.

20. Dom Theodore Ghesquiere, *Mathieu de Castro, premier vicaire apos-tolique aux Indes* (Louvain, 1937); Carlos Merces de Melo, S.J., *The Recruit-ment and Formation of the Native Clergy in India, 16th–19 Centuries: An Historico-Canonical Study* (Lisbon, 1955), pp. 215–53.

21. I think the remark was made by Norman Douglas, but I have mislaid the reference.

22. Donald Warren, Jr., "Portuguese Roots of Brazilian Spiritism," *Luso-Brazilian Review* 5 (Winter 1968): 3–33, is particularly perceptive on the attitude of the Portuguese Inquisition. Cf. also Rodney Gallop, *Portugal: A Book of Folk-ways* (Cambridge, 1936), pp. 49–185; A. H. de Oliveira Marques, *Daily Life in Portugal in the Late Middle Ages* (Madison, Wis., 1971), pp. 206–28. For the survival of folk religion and Black and White Magic elsewhere, see Gerald Strauss, "Success and Failure in the German Reformation," *Past and Present,* No. 67 (May 1975), pp. 30–63.

23. C. R. Boxer, "A Rare Luso-Brazilian Medical Treatise and Its Author: Luis Gomes Ferreira and His *Erario Mineral* of 1735 and 1755," *Indiana University Bookman,* No. 10, (November 1969), pp. 49–70, and idem, "A Footnote to Luis Gomes Ferreira, *Erario Mineral,* 1735 and 1755," *ibid.,* No. 11, (November 1973), pp. 89–92.

24. Pierre Duviols, *La Lutte contre les religions autochtones dans le Pérou colonial: "L'extirpation de l'idolatrie" entre 1532 et 1660* (Lima and Paris, 1971).

25. Ibid.

26. Jacques Lafaye, *Quetzalcóatl et Guadalupe: La formation de la con-science nationale au Mexique* (Paris, 1974), for the symbiosis of the Amerindian Aztec myth of Quetzalcóatl and the Spanish Christian myth of Guadalupe.

27. Georges Balandier, *Daily Life in the Kingdom of the Kongo from the 16th to the 18th Century* (New York, 1969); Randles, *L'Ancien Royaume du Congo.*

28. The fullest account is by L. Jadin, "Le Congo et la secte des Antoniens. Restauration du royaume sous Pedro IV et la 'Saint Antoine' Congolaise, 1694–1718," *Bulletin de l'Institut Historique Belge Rome,* fasc. 33 (Brussels, 1961), pp. 412–614. For shorter accounts based on this article, see L. Jadin, "Les sectes religeuses secretes des Antoniens au Congo, 1703–1709," *Cahiers des Religons Africaines,* 2 no. 3 (Kinshasa), (January 1968): 109–20; Balandier, *Daily Life in the Kingdom of the Kongo,* pp. 257–63.

29. João dos Santos, O.P., *Ethiopia Oriental* (Evora, 1609), pt. 2, bk. 2, chap. 13. On the culture of Monomotapa and its religious symbiosis see also Paul Schebesta, S.V.D., *Portugal's Konquistamission in S.O. Afrika* (Siegburg, 1966), especially pp. 44–53; M. D. D. Newitt, *Portuguese Settlement on the*

Zambesi: Exploration, Land Tenure, and Colonial Rule in East Africa (London, 1973); W. G. L. Randles, *L'Empire du Monomotapa du XVe au XIXe siècles* (Paris, 1975), oddly enough ignores the coronation ceremonies.

30. "Edital da Inquisição de Goa contra certos costumes e ritos da Africa Oriental," 21 January 1771, in J. H. da Cunha Rivara, ed., *O Chronista de Tissuary*, 4 vols. (Nova Goa, 1866–69), vol. 2, pp. 273–75. For similar syncretism between Muslim and Christian practices in eighteenth-century French Sengal, see J. D. Hargreaves, "Assimilation in 18th-century Senegal," *Journal of African History* 6 (1965): 177–84, and George E. Brooks, "The *Signares* of Saint-Louis and Goree: Women Entrepreneurs in Eighteenth-Century Senegal," in *Women in Africa: Studies in Social and Economic Change*, ed. Nancy J. Hafkin and Edna G. May (Stanford, Calif., 1976), pp. 19–44.

31. Inquisitor Antonio de Amaral Coutinho to the Crown, Goa, 26 January 1731, in J. H. da Cunha Rivara, *Ensaio Historico da Lingua Concani* (Nova Goa, 1858), pp. 354–56.

32. Phelan, *The Hispanization of the Philippines*, pp. 78–81; extracts from Tomas Ortiz, O.P., *Practica del ministerio* (Manila, 1731), in E. H. Blair and J. Robertson, eds., *The Philippine Islands*, 55 vols. (Cleveland, 1903–9), Vol. 43, pp. 103–112.

33. Gaspar da Cruz, O.P., *apud* C. R. Boxer, ed. and trans., *South China in the Sixteenth Century* Hakluyt Society, (London, 1953), pp. 51, 227.

34. John Leddy Phelan, *The Millennial Kingdom of the Franciscans in the New World,* 2nd revised ed., (Berkeley and Los Angeles, 1970), especially pp. 17–28, for the Joachimite-Spiritual Franciscan tradition; J. S. Cummins, "Christopher Columbus: Crusader, Visionary, and Servus Dei," in *Medieval Hispanic Studies Presented to Rita Hamilton,* ed. A. D. Deyermond (London, 1976), pp. 45–55.

35. See chapter 2, n. 26. Lockhart points out, on p. 10 of the article cited, that Spanish laymen were more ubiquitous and played a much larger part in the work of conversion than Ricard implies.

36. *Apud* Lewis Hanke, *The Spanish Struggle for Justice in the Conquest of America* (Madison, Wis., 1968), p. 51.

37. Antonio Vázquez de Espinosa, *Compendium and Description of the West Indies,* trans. Charles Upson Clark (Washington, D. C., 1942), p. 457.

38. Pierre Chaunu, *Conquête et exploitation des nouveaux mondes. XVIe siècle* (Paris, 1969), p. 399.

39. British Museum, Sloane Ms, 1572, fls. 58–60. I have not yet identified the anonymous author of this curious account, written in a clumsy Spanish.

40. *Apud* C. R. Boxer, *A Great Luso-Brazilien figure: Padre António Vieira, S.J., 1608–1697* (London, 1957, 1963), p. 12. The definitive work on this aspect of the many-sided Vieira is by Raymond Cantel, *Prophétisme et messianisme dans l'oeuvre d'António Vieira* (Paris, 1960). See also the interesting comparison of Vieira's millennial ideas with those of his Peruvian Creole contemporary, Fr. Gonzalo Tenorio, O.F.M., (1602–82?), in Phelan, *The Millennial Kingdom of the Franciscans,* pp. 122–25.

41. Further details on Queiroz's millennial ideas in C. R. Boxer, "Faith and Empire: The Cross and the Crown in Portuguese Expansion, 15th–18th Centuries," *Terrae Incognitae* (1976): 73–89. For similar outpourings in seventeenth-century England see J. G. A. Pocock, "Time, History, and Eschatology in the Thought of Thomas Hobbes," in *The Diversity of History: Essays in Honour of Sir Herbert Butterfield,* ed. J. H. Elliott and H. G. Koningsberger (New York, 1970), pp. 149–98; R. W. Southern, "Aspects of the European Tradition of Historical Writing: 3. History as Prophecy," *Transactions of the Royal Historical Society,* 5th Series, vol. 22 (London, 1972), pp. 159–80, especially pp. 177–80.

42. Roberto Gulbenkian, (ed. and trans.), *L'Ambassade en Perse de Luis Pereira de Lacerda, et des Pères Portugais de l'Ordre de Saint Augustin, 1604–1605* (Lisbon, 1972), and the review by Pierre Oberling in the *Journal of Asian History* 8 (1974): 52–56.

43. Ignacio de Santa Teresa, "Estado do presente Estado da India," Goa, 1725, *apud* Boxer, *The Portuguese Seaborne Empire,* p. 374.

44. Warren, Jr., "Portuguese Roots of Brazilian Spiritism," pp. 3–33.

45. Thomas V. Cohen, "Why the Jesuits Joined, 1540–1600," *Canadian Historical Papers* (December 1974), pp. 237–57. We need much more statistical work on these lines, if the documentation is available. This article does not deal with Portuguese and Spaniards.

46. *Thomas Gage's Travels in the New World,* ed., J. Eric S. Thompson (Norman, Okla., 1958). For the 15,000 Jesuit volunteers, see John Correia-Afonso, S.J., "Indo-American Contacts through Jesuit Missionaries" (Paper read at the thirtieth International Congress of Human Sciences in Asia and North Africa, Mexico City, 3–8 August, 1976; in press).

47. One of many such instances was Fr. Juan Pobre de Zamora, who, after serving as a soldier under the Duke of Alva in Flanders, became a Franciscan lay-brother and a tireless missionary in the Far East, 1594–1615.

48. Josef Wicki, S.J., "Liste der Jesuiten-Indien fahrer, 1541–1758," in Hans Flasche, ed., *Portugiesische Forschungen der Görresgesellschaft. Aufsätze zur Portugiesischen Kulturgeschichte,* vol. 7 (Munster and Westfalen, 1967), pp. 252–450, especially pp. 332–34.

49. Philip Caraman, S.J., *The Lost Paradise: An Account of the Jesuits in Paraguay, 1607–1768* (London, 1975), p. 277.

50. *The Travels of Peter Mundy, 1608–1667,* vol. 3, pt. 1, *1634–1637* (London, 1919), p. 164.

Bibliographical Index

The following index contains the names of authors of books and articles, with the titles of collections of documents and other items. The number after a name refers to the page in the Notes where an author's work is mentioned. Any additional numbers refer to other works by the same author.

General Index

Library of Congress Cataloging in Publication Data

Boxer, Charles Ralph, 1904–
    The Church Militant and Iberian Expansion, 1440–1770.

    (The Johns Hopkins symposia in comparative history; no. 10)
    Given as the James S. Schouler Lectures, Mar. 1976.
    Includes bibliographical references and index.
    1. Catholic Church in Spain—History—Addresses, essays, lectures. 2. Catholic Church in Portugal—History—Addresses, essays, lectures. I. Title. II. Series.
BX1584.B68   282'.46   77–18386
ISBN O–8018–2042–1